Traditional Italian Cuisine

FROM PUGLIA WITH FLAVOR

Family Secrets in 50+1 Apulian Recipes. From Gargano, to Itria Valley, to Salento, the True Flavors of the Apulian Mediterranean Diet.

Aurora Zito
Karing Ship

To My Father
and to all my „Martinese" relatives.
Those who are still there and those
Who are no longer.

© **Copyright: Aurora Zito & Karing Ship 2022 - All rights reserved**

The contents of this book may not be reproduced, duplicated or transmitted without the direct written permission of the authors or publisher.

This book is copyrighted and intended for personal use only. You may not modify, distribute, sell, or otherwise use individual parts or the contents in their entirety of this book without the consent of the author or publisher. Only brief quotations for review purposes and/or citations on Blogs and Web sites are permitted, with the requirement that the source be indicated. Free use is permitted for Public Domain and Creative Commons images only (under the terms of the respective licenses indicated in the endnotes).

Disclaimer

Please note that the information contained in this document is for informational and entertainment purposes only. Every effort has been made to present accurate, reliable, and complete information. No warranty of any kind is stated or implied. By reading this document, the reader agrees that in no event shall the authors and the publisher be liable for any damages or losses, direct or indirect, incurred as a result of the use of the information contained in the book, including but not limited to, - errors, omissions or inaccuracies and to what is stated on external sites whose links are cited. In particular, it is the sole responsibility of readers to verify that they have no allergies and/or intolerances to each of the ingredients mentioned in this book. By continuing reading you accept all of the conditions described above.

Table of Contents

Table of Contents..4
Introduction..6
Mussel Recipes..11
    Mussel Soup..12
    Arraganate (Grated) Mussels..14
    Stuffed Mussels "Alla Tarantina"..16
    Rice, Potatoes and Mussels. AKA the Original "Tiella Barese"....................18
    Fried Mussels..20
Bread, Pizza & Co..22
    The Fried Panzerotto..23
    The Rustic from Lecce..25
    U p'zz'tidd' - Focaccia with Onions and Olives..27
    A F'cazz' - AKA the typical Pugliese Focaccia with potatoes.....................29
    The Pittule Salentine..31
    The Puccia Pugliese (or Salentina)...33
    I Frisedd' - AKA the Pugliese "Friselle" or "Frise".......................................35
First Courses..37
    Orecchiette and Turnip Greens - (I Strasc'net')..38
    Orecchiette Cozze e Fagioli...40
    Orecchiette (or Cavatelli) with Burrata and Sundried Tomatoes in Oil......42
    Pasta with Tomatoes, Eggplant and Black Olives.......................................43
    Troccoli alla Foggiana..45
    Minchiaredd' e Pulupitt' (Minchiareddi and Meatballs) with Tomato Sauce......47
    Orecchiette with Green Beans and Cacioricotta Cheese.............................50
    Pasta with Ricotta Forte..51
    Pasta coi Cicer' (Chickpeas)...52
    Cavatelli with Cardoncelli Mushrooms (and Sausage)................................54
    Pasta with Urchins...56
    Orecchiette with Sardines and Turnip Greens..57
Vegetable and Meatless Dishes..59
    The Stuffed Eggplants (I Marangèll' Chièn')...60
    Puglia Style Eggplant Parmigiana..62
    Fried Lampascioni...64
    Stuffed Fried Zucchini Flowers..66
    Eggplant Meatballs (Fried or Baked)...68
    Breadballs (with Eggs)...70
    The Mashed Broad Beans..71
    Eggs and Sponsali Onions (Ciambotto)..73
    Crouton Foggia-style with Provola (or Caciocavallo cheese).....................74
    Onions of Acquaviva...75
Meat Main Courses...77
    Braised Gnumm'riedd'..78
    The Bombette (small Bombs) from Martina Franca....................................80
    Cervellata with Sauce..82

    I Vraciulidd' - (The Braciòle) 83
    Agnellone al Forno con i Lampascioni (Lamb in the oven with Lampascioni) 85
    The Chicken "Cusutu 'Nculu" - AKA, Stuffed Chicken 87
Fish Main Courses 89
    Octopus in Pignatta 90
    Anchovies Tarantine style 91
    Gratinated Anchovies 93
    Gallipoli's Scapece 94
    Braised Eel (or Capitone) 95
Holiday Sweets 96
    Le Cartellate (I Cartiedd') 97
    Easter Taralli 99
    Purceddhri 101
    The Intorchiate 103
    Mostaccioli (Mustazzule) 105
Notes 108
About the Authors 109
    Aurora Zito 109
    Karing Ship 109
Other Italian Cookbook from the same Publisher 110

Introduction

Although I was not born there, in Apulia are my origins and since my earliest childhood I have breathed its scents, tasted its flavors, and enjoyed all the now well-known "beauties" that this region can offer.

My dad was from Martina Franca, in the Itria Valley - yes, the one with so many „Trulli" in the countryside and with the three "White Cities" (Martina Franca, Locorotondo and Cisternino) that form the apexes of its triangle - and thanks to an endless kinship (not to mention friends and acquaintances), Apulian cuisine practically has no secrets for me. Not only that: most of the recipes I have been lucky enough to enjoy, since the early sixties were prepared and cooked by people born and raised at the beginning of the 20th century and thus, still totally anchored in the old peasant traditions. Their recipes weren't "Cool" in those days, but just the everyday preparations. On the tables of my countless aunts and certain cousins (even older or the same age as my father, who was born in the early 1920s) appeared every day those delicacies of the "poor" and "mediterranean" cuisine that then, with mass tourism and (sigh) globalization, have now become "musts" of "trendy" restaurants and clubs.

A colorful note: back then, in the early 1960s, there were practically no restaurants in Martina Franca (maybe one, in a cheap little hotel) and no pizzerias either. In fact who went to restaurants then? People prepared and ate at home! Perhaps the only "concession" was the so-called "Fornello Pronto" of many butcher shops. What was it? You will find out later, reading the meat recipes.

I have to admit that, despite the enormous changes in the Society, compared to those times, the Pugliese culinary tradition still holds up well to the advance of progress and there are many places where you can enjoy excellent and still (almost) uncontaminated recipes. I have been able to personally test this many times, thanks to my collaborations with travel or food and wine magazines.

So, why write a cookbook of Apulian dishes today?

I had actually never thought about it but, perhaps because of the upheavals caused in our lives by recent "epidemiological" events, I realized how fleeting and random a certain lifestyle is. Any day now you can find yourself from traveling the length and breadth of the world, to the most rigid confinement within four walls. And maybe not even "your" four walls! You literally can no longer reach out to places, friends and family.

And what do you do then? If not cling to one's interests, passions, memories and traditions? As we have seen, many of the "confined" people have taken to cooking in an almost unbridled way. Home baking has taken over and (albeit aided by modern technology) has brought families back to savoring the taste of freshly made bread again.

In short, a series of "healthy habits" that many of us have rediscovered and hopefully will not lose again too easily. Let's say that cooking well (and the healthiest possible way) can be considered one of the very few positive side effects of our forced "imprisonments."

So, when the Publisher told me about this project, I eagerly joined in. Indeed, I said to myself, why not make all those little "secrets" of my family tradition available to everyone? Why not let cooking enthusiasts and foodies know, how my Aunt Barbara prepared Orecchiette or my cousin Carmela prepared "Pizzitello"? How not (try at least) to let readers breathe in those magical atmospheres that I breathed since early childhood?

As the great Marcel Proust teaches, from the taste and scent of a simple treat (a Madeleine) can even be born monumental literary works such as the "Recherche."[1]

Food, emotions, memories, are all intimately connected in our minds, even if often, they remain hidden in the subconscious. But all it takes is precisely a scent--and they come back powerfully before us. People, places, events return, and we realize that we have experienced so many things, even if we no longer remember them.

Therefore, I hope to succeed, with this book, to offer those who do not yet know it, the chance to experience Traditional Apulian Cuisine as seen by an "Insider"-while for those who already know it-the intent is to bring back a memory: perhaps of a good trip, a happy moment, a beautiful place or ... an emotion.

Note:

The main secret of Pugliese Cuisine is the quality of the ingredients. Therefore, to make the recipes that I will propose, I strongly recommend using (at least as much as possible) the elements of Apulian origin. *Nowadays it is not difficult to find them in the best grocery stores or markets. Even easier, thanks to technology, is to order them on the Web and have them shipped to you.*

There is a colossal difference in fact between using (for example) aged "Cacioricotta" Cheese to grate instead of another, albeit excellent, cheese. The same goes for Extra Virgin Olive Oil (EVO) (choose if you can, the one from Bitonto), "Col Pizzo" Tomatoes, Mozzarelle (nodini) or Burrata from Andria, Altamura Bread etc. Then let's not talk about the Mussels, which should be strictly from Taranto or at least ... from other coastal areas of the region (the ones from Savelletri are excellent). If I indicate "Wine" in the recipes, however, the aroma of a heavenly Barolo cannot replace those of wines made from local grape varieties such as Primitivo di Manduria, Negroamaro, Nero di Troia or Malvasia. It is a matter...philological! The ingredients of every dish (not just Apulian ones) like dialects have a different "sound" depending on where they come from. Soil, air, rainfall, methods of cultivation, harvesting and preparation make a difference even if the ingredient formally is the same.

All this I emphasize for the sole purpose of bringing back to you the true essence of Pugliese food. Not that elements from different areas, are not good in themselves.

I also recommend you, with all my heart, not to use blatantly "Fake" Italian ingredients such as, for example, Parmesan Cheese or certain Mozzarellas of dubious origin... and also potentially harmful to your health.

If you want to cook Italian (and especially Apulian) you must use original basic ingredients. Most of these are guaranteed by the DOP, IGP, PAT marks (which cover foods or products such as Extra Virgin Olive Oil (EVO), Parmigiano Reggiano, certain Salumi etc.) or DOC, DOCG, IGT, IGP which are reserved for Wines.

Regarding meats, seafoods and fishes, if not available fresh, you can use the original frozen ones, or the equivalent local ones in your country.

Above: The „TRUE" Parmigiano Reggiano with the D.O.P. mark on it

Another note.

I often happened to find on various blogs or cookbooks some recipes of "Typical Pugliese" dishes based for example, on... Salmon (sic!) or other similar amenities. But can you imagine my grandma in 1935, preparing a nice slice of Salmon for dinner?

W.t.f.? My grandmother did not even know what Salmon was! There are no Salmon in Apulia... It's not like we're in Alaska! Instead, she would prepare a nice pan of Mussels, which my grandfather would bring home on his way back from his job in Taranto!

So be careful what you "find" around and think carefully if, certain ingredients, can really be counted among those used in Traditional Apulian Cuisine.

In this cookbook, I am not going to offer you a huge number of recipes, just to make this book seem more important, nor am I going to fill these pages with lots of beautiful colorful photographs and poor "substance" that would unnecessarily increase its price. Much less will I be here to bore you with nutritional values and calorie tables, because the fact that the "Mediterranean diet" is one of the healtiest is known by now even to stones. The important thing is (as always) not to overdo the quantities and thus consume foods in moderation. The ones I offer in this book instead are "definitely" Traditional recipes and not the result of the (albeit laudable) imagination of some "trendy" modern-day Chef. In this case, the saying "Few but Good" applies more than ever! Although (of course) every Apulian who will read this book will have something to say about this or that dish (and this "variety" is the beauty of Italy) I will reveal my little "Family Secrets" and if made with the right ingredients (see above) you can be sure that the dishes you will prepare will have the "real" flavors and aromas of Apulia.

Mussel Recipes

(I put Mussel recipes first in this book because their use is so widespread in Apulia that, with Mussels, you can make an entire meal! They go well as appetizers, first courses or main courses... It's funny that they don't make desserts with them too!)

Mussel Soup

Simple, yet extraordinary and very tasty, mussel soup is a must-have dish in Apulian cuisine. Indeed, there is no self-respecting "Pugliese" who does not love this dish. Of all of them, Taranto Mussels, bred in the Mar Piccolo, are the favorite, but of course, if you don't have them on hand, don't worry: the recipe is so good that any type of Mussels will do, as long as they are of safe provenance. It is prepared quickly and easily and should be enjoyed together with bruscato bread cut into cubes.

Difficulty: Easy - Preparation: Quick - Cost: Moderate

What You Need (for 4 people):
- Mussels: 3,5/4,5 lb
- 1,1 lb of fresh tomatoes (we suggest the classic Apulian „col pizzo" tomatoes, or succulent Pachino's „datterini" or „cherry" tomatoes from Sicily). Failing that, peeled tomatoes, such as San Marzano, can be used.
- 1 Shallot (or 1 Onion)
- Extra Virgin Olive Oil (EVO). Apulian, of course!
- 1 Dried Chili Pepper
- Parsley
- Celery

How to Prepare:
- First, wash the mussels well by scrubbing them with a small brush. A classic one made of beech wood is preferable.
- Clean the tomatoes and cut them into four parts.
- In a saucepan or frying pan of good diameter, sauté a chopped mixture of shallot/onion, parsley and celery.
- Pour the tomatoes into the sauté and let them go on high heat for a few minutes, taking care to stir often.

- When the tomatoes have softened, add the mussels and put a lid on the casserole (or pan). In a few minutes, the shells will open due to the heat and the water released will form a tasty sauce joining the sauté and tomatoes.

- Once all the mussels have opened, you can add a pinch of finely chopped chili pepper to taste and let everything sit for 5 minutes.

- At this point, serve the soup nice and hot on the table along with the bread croutons, which you will have prepared in the meantime.

Arraganate (Grated) Mussels

Here is another "staple" of popular Apulian cuisine. In fact, thanks to the long coastal expanses, the art of farming these tasty mussels has always been developed in Apulia. From the Gargano promontory in the north to the extreme tip of Salento in the south, mussel dishes appear very often on Apulian tables.

Difficulty: Easy/Medium* - Preparation: Quick - Cost: Moderate

What You Need (for 4 people):
  - Mussels: 3,5/4,5 lb (possibly from Taranto)
  - 6,3 oz of grated Pecorino Cheese
  - Breadcrumbs: 6,3 oz
  - 2 cloves of Garlic
  - Parsley
  - Extra Virgin Olive Oil (EVO) - do I really have to say it? Possibly Apulian!
  - 2 Eggs
  - Ground Pepper
  - Salt

How to Prepare:
  - First clean the mussels well, washing them thoroughly under water and scrubbing them with a small brush (it is preferable to use the special one, made of beech wood).
  - Now you will need to open the mussels one by one. (*If you have never done this before, I strongly recommend watching some appropriate tutorials on the Web. After the first few mussels you will definitely be able to do it the best you can and--without hurting yourself with the knife.*) After opening them, discard the part of the shells that does not contain the fruit and arrange the others in a baking dish or dish.
  - After opening and beating the eggs a bit in a bowl or deep dish (depending on how you are used to it), add the well-washed, dried and finely chopped Parsley leaves along with a generous dose of Ground Pepper.
  - In another bowl, prepare a mixture with the Breadcrumbs, a pinch of salt, the finely minced garlic and the Extra Virgin Oil (4 or 5 tablespoons - adjust so that the consistency is neither too fluid nor too compact).

- Now pour the contents of the first bowl, dividing it among the various mussels, then top each one with the breadcrumb mixture.

- You can now place in the oven (at 390 °F) for about 20 minutes.

- Once they are done cooking, remove them from the oven and leave a few minutes at room temperature. Then, you can serve them on the table--to the great happiness of the diners.

Stuffed Mussels "Alla Tarantina"

One more recipe based on Mussels, which we Apulians never get bored with... This time we prepare them Stuffed, according to the tradition of Taranto, whose farms of these mussels are, since time immemorial, known and appreciated all over the world.

Difficulty: Easy - Preparation: Quick - Cost: Moderate

What You Need (For 4 people):

- Mussels: 3,5/4,5 lb - Tarantine? Yep... *ça va sans dire!*
- 1 Egg
- Dry Bread: 10,6 oz
- 1,6 lb of Pelati (peeled tomatoes), but a ready-made Sauce will also do. Of course, if you have the time and inclination, the ideal would be to use fresh tomatoes, such as Apulian "Col Pizzo" tomatoes, or Pachino's cherry/date tomatoes.
- Grated Pecorino Cheese: 1,8 oz
- Extra Virgin Olive Oil (EVO). I know, I'm repeating myself, but what do you do...won't you use the Pugliese one?
- Parsley
- Garlic (a couple of cloves)
- Ground Pepper
- Salt

How to Prepare:

- As always, first wash the mussels well, cleaning their shells with a beechwood brush. As an alternative you can use a well-cleaned kitchen straws.
- Then put the mussels in a pan together with a clove of garlic and a couple of tablespoons of Extra Virgin Olive Oil (EVO). After 3-4 minutes on the stove the shells will be open just enough to prepare our recipe.
- Now prepare a sauce: put another pan on the stove with 3-4 tablespoons of Extra Virgin Oil, the other clove of garlic and the peeled tomatoes (or ready-made sauce) and bring it to a boil.

- Meanwhile, strain through a strainer the liquid from the mussels you had opened.

- Soak the stale bread in warm water and then mix it (after squeezing it well) together with the Pecorino Cheese, Egg, and Parsley (well washed, squeezed and chopped very finely). Also add a bit of the filtered liquid from the mussels. Be careful not to make the mixture too soft. If necessary, add more bread or cheese.

- Now, with this mixture, fill the partially opened Mussels one by one, taking care not to overdo it. Then tie them up using twine or a kitchen rubber band.

- Place the Mussels in the sauce, to which you will also have added the remainder of the Mussels' water, and cook over medium heat for about twenty minutes.

- The dish is ready... Enjoy!

Rice, Potatoes and Mussels. AKA the Original "Tiella Barese"

In a land of "Parochialism" and dialects as Italy is, obviously Puglia is no exception. This is why interpretations (and names) of this symbolic recipe vary from country to country. If in Salento they call it "Taieddrha" while in Bari they say "Tièdda" it matters little to us, however. The important thing is that it is made following a traditional recipe, so we are on the safe side.

Difficulty: Medium- Preparation: Medium- Cost: Moderate

What You Need (For 4 people):

- Rice: 10,5 oz - It should be strictly of the "Carnaroli" variety, due to its absorption qualities. If you want to learn more about some of the best rices produced in Italy, we definitely recommend reading this Special Article[s] Dedicated to 5 Top Italian Companies!
- Mussels: 4,4/6,6 lb - Whatever, don't look at me like that...I'll say it anyway: from Taranto!
- Tomatoes (Col Pizzo or Pachino's): 0,5 lb
- Two Onions.
- Potatoes. The choice can be yellow or red ones. Both very suitable for baking. 2.2 lb may be enough.
- During the summer you can make a variation by adding 2 or 3 fresh zucchini.
- 1,5 oz of grated Pecorino Cheese.
- Pugliese EVO oil (unfailing of course).
- Garlic, Salt and Pepper.

How to Prepare:

- After the usual washing and cleaning of the Mussels, they should be opened "raw," with a small knife. As mentioned above, we recommend watching some Video Tutorials on the net if you are not handy. Store the water leaking from the Mussels in a jar and then filter it. Deposit the Mussels in an appropriate container.
- In an earthenware "baking dish" (if you do not have one, you can use one of those made of aluminum but...be careful, you are going out of Tradition) pour a bit of Extra Virgin Olive Oil (EVO) and compose a first layer of Onions, which you have previously cut into thin slices.

- Next, a layer of Potatoes, again cut into thin slices. Eventually, add also some zucchini slices (only in Summer), some cherry tomatoes cut in half and sprinkle with chopped Parsley.

- Sprinkle with a layer of Pecorino cheese, Ground Pepper and some Oil.

- Now it is finally the turn of the Mussels. Lay them all next to each other (the shells go on the bottom) and then cover with the Rice. On top, place the remaining rounds of Onion and sprinkle everything with a clove of minced garlic, Pecorino, Ground Pepper and Oil.

- When finished, cover everything well with more Potato slices. Sprinkle again with Pecorino, put the remaining Tomatoes and a further layer of Oil.

- Now prepare about half a liter of salted water, dissolving 0,12 oz of salt in warm water. Then add the filtered Mussel water. Mix well and pour it carefully into the "Tiella," near the edge, so that it comes flush with the last layer of Potatoes.

- While preheating the oven to 390 °F, keep the tiella on low heat. When the oven is ready, put it in the oven and let it bake for 50 to 70 minutes. To adjust, you can observe the crust that will form on the surface.

- When cooked, let the Tiella sit at room temperature for a few minutes and serve it warm to your guests who will surely be eagerly waiting and drooling at this point!

Fried Mussels

I conclude the chapter devoted to Mussels with a recipe for Fried Mussels, which, in the historical memory of my (big) family, have a special place. This is both because of the frequency they were prepared in the past, but also because of an anecdote that even revealed their "thaumaturgic" qualities. *Btw. Don't do this at home of course! I'm just kidding!* :-)

In fact, the story goes that an uncle of mine (then a child) having fallen ill with Typhoid fever, had to go through a long period of almost total fasting. In those days, there were no antibiotics and during his convalescence he could only take milk. You can well imagine how such a thing was almost more harmful (especially psychologically) than the disease itself. Well, one night driven by his now excruciating hunger, he sneaked up, went into the kitchen and devoured the first thing he found in the pantry: a half-pan of... Fried Mussels left over from the night before! The next morning he was perfectly well--perfectly healed!

Difficulty: Medium- Preparation: Medium- Cost: Content

What You Need:

- Calculate at least 4 or 5 Mussels per person (even up to twice as many if you are going to use them as a main course instead of an appetizer/stuzzichino). Mussels should be as large as possible and of course from-well, you already know it!
- Extra Virgin Olive Oil (EVO)
- Breadcrumbs
- 2 or 3 Eggs (depends on the above)
- Flour
- Salt

How to Prepare:

- Wash and clean the Mussels well and open them with a small knife (see previous recipes).
- Remove the fruits and dry them well on paper towels.
- Beat the Eggs in a bowl.

- Dip the individual Mussels first in the Flour (shake off the excess) then in the Eggs and finally in the Breadcrumbs.

- Fry them a few minutes in a pan with nice hot Evo Oil. When the surface is golden brown, remove them from the pan with a skimmer and deposit them on top of a tray with paper towels. Salt lightly and there you go, your "medicine" is ready!

Bread, Pizza & Co.

The Fried Panzerotto

Even in the case of the typical Pugliese Panzerotto we have several variations, all due to individual local and even more, family traditions. For example, there are those who use Semola rimacinata for the dough, those who use only 00 flour and those who use a 50-50 mix of both. Then let's not talk about leavening techniques or filling components. I have decided to keep it "simple" so that everyone can find the necessary ingredients and prepare in a way that is not too complicated. But rest assured...a Panzerotto is still a Panzerotto and that is: delicious!

Difficulty: Medium- Preparation: Medium- Cost: Moderate

What You Need (For 4 people):

For the Dough:
- 1,6 lb 00 Flour
- Yeast - ¾ of a cube
- Water – 10,8 fl oz
- Salt

For the Filling:
- 10,6 oz of Italian Mozzarella
- Tomato Sauce
- Ground Pepper
- Grated Parmigiano Reggiano DOP

How to Prepare:

- First, you will need to prepare the dough. Then heat the Water with a pinch of Salt and place the Flour on top of a work surface (if you have a "pastry board" even better) to form a hollowed out cone in the center. Inside put a teaspoon of Sugar and the crumbled Brewer's Yeast. Still in the center of the cone pour in the heated water and start kneading.

- When the dough has reached a smooth and homogeneous consistency, place it in a container, taking care to cover it with a cloth and leave it for at least a couple of hours in a warm place. In winter near a radiator and in summer near a window exposed to the sun.

- After the rising time has elapsed, divide the mass into two/three parts and shape it into a cylinder. Help yourself with a little flour on the work surface and on your hands to keep it from sticking. Following this, cut the cylinders into a number of discs. The size and quantity will depend on what size you want to give your Panzerotti. Then flatten the disks with a rolling pin until you get small "pizzas" with a diameter of 6 to 7,8 in

- Meanwhile, while the dough was rising, you will have pepared the filling. That is, you will have cut the Mozzarella into small cubes and mixed it with the Tomato Sauce and a pinch of Salt and Pepper (this is optional) so as to obtain a homogeneous mixture.

- Now, lay some of this mixture in the center of each of the dough discs, taking care to drain the mozzarella/tomato mixture well to prevent it from leaking out during cooking. For the same reason, do not overdo the amount.

- Close the Panzerotto forming a crescent and carefully seal the edges with fingers greased with Olive Oil or a fork. Then trim the same edges with a pastry wheel.

- Now all that remains is to fry the Panzerotti in plenty of boiling EVO Oil, turning them on both sides until they take on a golden color. In all, 3-4 minutes at most will be enough.

- Remove the Panzerotti from the Oil with a skimmer and place them on a tray on which you have arranged a generous layer of Kitchen Paper, to let them dry. Then, you can safely start ... devouring them!

You can experiment with many variations for the filling, using different combinations of Scamorza, Caciocavallo, Spicy Salami, Capers, Anchovies and even meat and vegetables such as Peppers, Turnip Greens, Mushrooms and Sausage. Let me tell you, though: a „Classic" Panzerotto is priceless! For everything else there is... a Credit Card! :-)

The Rustic from Lecce

In a very broad sense, we can define this specialty as a "variant" of Panzerotto. But in this case puff pastry is used and they are baked in the oven. Then, it's just a matter of filling them as you like. The classic filling is obviously Tomato and Mozzarella, but again you can experiment (for example with Ricotta Forte) at will. Then, if you happen to be in Lecce, you will easily find it in the city's fry shops/restaurants.

Difficulty: Easy - Preparation: Quick - Cost: Moderate

What You Need (Serves for 6 Rustici):
 - I'm going to make a "Break from the norm," and to make a long story short, I recommend getting ready-made Puff Pastry. - One Roll (about 9 oz).
 - Peeled Tomatoes - 1 large
 - Italian Mozzarella – 1,4 oz
 - Extra Virgin Olive Oil (EVO)
 - 1 Egg
 - Béchamel sauce – 1.8 oz
 - Garlic (1 clove)
 - Salt
 - Ground Pepper
 - Oregano

How to Prepare:
 - Roll out the puff pastry and divide it into 12 equal parts (square or round), helping yourself with the appropriate metal molds.
 - In a pan with a little EVO Oil, sauté the Peeled Garlic, a pinch of Salt, a pinch of Oregano and a sprinkling of Pepper, then add the Peeled Tomato in pieces. Let it simmer for about 15 minutes.
 - Cut the Mozzarella into pieces, drain it and mix it with the Béchamel.
 - Open the Egg in a deep dish and beat it well. Then, with a kitchen brush, spread 6 pieces of Puff Pastry.
 - Place some of the Mozzarella and Béchamel mixture in the center of the 6 parts just coated with the Egg and add a little bit of the Tomato Sauce.

- Close the shapes with the 6 remaining parts, seal the edges well with your fingers (or use a fork) and then brush the surface with the remaining of the Beaten Egg.

- Bake at about 370 °F (if you have a fan oven it is better set it at 356 °F) for about 20 minutes, until the Rustici are lightly browned.

- Take them out and let them cool for a few minutes before consuming.

U p'zz'tidd' - Focaccia with Onions and Olives.

If I had to choose just one among the various focaccias, pizzas and other similar products, probably U p'zz'tidd' (translated: the Pizzitello) would be in first place! For me, this focaccia is evocative of the memories, flavors and scents of childhood: it is the essence of the Itria Valley. I will offer it to you with a little "Secret" from my family tradition (this is how my cousin Carmela prepared it): a secret that will make the difference.

Difficulty: Medium - Preparation: Medium - Cost: Low

What You Need (For 4 people):

For the dough:
- 00 Flour – 2,2 lb
- Brewer's yeast - 1 sachet
- Warm water
- 4 Small boiled potatoes
- Salt

For the Filling:
- Fresh spring onions (called Spunzel') to taste.
- Pitted black olives
- Extra Virgin Olive Oil (EVO) (EVO)
- Salt
- Anchovies in oil (the Secret I told you about)

How to Prepare:
- First peel and boil the Potatoes. Once ready, mash them.
- Dissolve the Yeast in a glass of warm water with a teaspoon of sugar.
- Combine the Flour, Potatoes and the liquid with the yeast, then knead until the dough is smooth and firm. Place the mass in a bowl, cover it tightly with a cloth and let it rise until the dough has doubled in volume.

- While the dough is rising, you can prepare the filling: place the well-washed and sliced spring onions in a saucepan with EVO oil and a bit of water. Let them simmer for about 10 minutes.

- Now add the Olives and a couple of pickled Anchovies. Let them cook for another 10 minutes.

- When the dough has risen sufficiently divide it in two. Flatten the two parts with a rolling pin and lay one inside a baking pan about 30 cm in diameter that you have previously oiled.

- Pour the now-cooled spring onions over the layer of dough in the baking dish and cover it with the other half of the dough. try to join the edges well around the entire circumference and then cover everything with a thin layer of EVO oil.

- Place the pan in a preheated oven at about 440 °F for between 25 and 35 minutes. A good indicator of baking is the light browning of the surface.

- When done, remove the pan and let it cool. U p'zz'tiedd' is at its best when enjoyed at room temperature. Be warned, though: it is "addictive."

A F'cazz' - AKA the typical Pugliese Focaccia with potatoes.

Strictly quite high and soft! That's right, because A F'cazz' with potatoes is made to be stuffed with mortadella - or salami - and mozzarella cheese (possibly the classic "nodini" originally from Andria, but you can find them now in any dairy in any Apulian town). You can also replace the mozzarella with the famous "Ricotta Squanta," for an even more intense and distinctive taste.

Even this focaccia cannot fail to remind me of so many summer dinners outdoors, under a starry sky, with "oceanic" gatherings of relatives in the square in front of my Aunt's Grazia large Trulli group, while from the wood-burning oven cousins Carmela (another one...) and Rosina churned out pans upon pans of this delicacy. Now maybe in New York, Paris, Milan or Tokyo there will not be Trulli and probably, not even a wood-fired oven, but I will try to make sure that you will not miss them too much, wherever you are. In fact... you will feel (and taste) like you were there too.

Difficulty: Easy - Preparation: Medium - Cost: Content

What You Need (For a 30-cm baking pan):
  - 8,8 oz of Remilled Semolina
  - 00 flour: 12,3 oz
  - Brewer's yeast - 1 loaf of about 0,7 oz
  - 7 oz Potatoes (yellow dough)
  - 15 "Col Pizzo" or cherry tomatoes
  - Extra Virgin Olive Oil (EVO)
  - Oregano (either fresh or dried is fine)
  - Water – 12 oz
  - Salt

How to Prepare:
- Form the "classic" cone of Flour and add the Semolina and Potatoes, which you will have previously boiled and mashed.
  - Prepare 8,4 oz of lukewarm water in which you will dissolve the Beer Yeast.
  - Start kneading the mixture by adding the water with the yeast a little at a time. Also add a pinch of Salt.

- When the dough has reached a certain consistency (it should not be too soft and sticky), take the baking pan and grease it with EVO Oil. As an alternative to the Oil, you can use a sheet of baking paper. Then spread the dough all over the surface. Cover it with a cloth and let it rest, in a warm, dry place for at least 3 to 4 hours.

- While the focaccia is rising, cut the tomatoes in half and press them lightly to remove the seeds.

- Also prepare an emulsion with 1,7 oz of EVO oil and 3,4 oz of water, with which you will sprinkle the surface of your F'cazz' at the end of preparation

- At the end of the rising process, grease your fingers with Extra Virgin Oil and first, compact the dough well in the baking pan, then with your fingers, make small hollows on its surface. Into each of these insert half a cherry tomato.

- Now sprinkle the surface with a the salt and oregano to taste. Then evenly distribute the water/oil emulsion prepared earlier.

- Now all that remains is to bake at 430/450 °F for 30 to 35 minutes. When you see that the tomatoes are caramelized and the surface light browned, then it means it is ready to be taken out of the oven.

- Let it rest for a few minutes and then cut it into large wedges, which you will serve on the table in a large soup tureen.

The Pittule Salentine

I won't bore you here with yet another list of lexical variations, but-for those who don't yet know-these very simple "balls" of fried dough are a staple of Salento cuisine! Absolutely impossible in fact, to define them simplistically among appetizers, side dishes or desserts... because they are actually all of these at once, thanks to their incredible versatility. In fact, you can accompany them with Tomatoes or vegetables, stuff them with fillings as you like, or enjoy them as they are instead of Bread. Needless to emphasize then that anyone who tries them returns from Salento in withdrawal. (The servings below are for 6 people - but it really depends on how you want to use them. You could even make an entire meal out of Pittule).

Difficulty: Easy - Preparation: Medium - Cost: Content

What You Need:

- 00 Flour: 1,65 lb
- Brewer's yeast - 1 loaf (about 0,7 oz)
- Water: 20,3 oz
- Sugar
- Salt
- Frying oil

How to Prepare:

- Prepare the yeast by dissolving it in a little warm water and adding the Sugar (two teaspoons). Stir well.
- Now sift the Flour into a large mixing bowl and add a pinch of Salt and the water with the Yeast starting to mix well. Gradually add the rest of the water, which you will also have warmed.
- When the mixture has reached a certain consistency begin to knead it with some "vigor" and beat it occasionally on the work surface. In this way it will absorb that air that will give the Pittule their final "fluffy" texture.

- At some point, air bubbles will appear on the surface of the dough. This is the right time to let it rise (well covered, in a warm place) until the dough reaches twice its initial volume.

- Place a large pan (the edges should be high) with plenty of Frying Oil on the stove.

- You are now faced with a choice: form walnut-sized balls and fry them directly like this, or place inside them any of the countless possible fillings (see below) that you will have decided on.

- With wet fingers and/or helping yourself with a spoon, then form the balls and put them to fry in nice hot Oil for a few minutes. As soon as they take on a nice golden color you can drain them and place them on paper towels.

- Like any self-respecting fried food, they should be served immediately.

I suggest here just a few (the rest is up to your imagination) of the possible fillings for your fragrant Pittule:

Fish Meat, Shrimp or Cod (previously boiled and shredded).

Boiled Turnip Greens or other vegetables.

Ricotta (regular, or better, the characteristic Ricotta Squanta Pugliese).

Chopped dried tomatoes in oil.

Creams, Chocolate or various jams.

The Puccia Pugliese (or Salentina)

Particularly popular in the south-central part of the region, it has become a must in modern cuisine. In these times of Street & Finger Food, it's particularly suited to satisfy anyone's needs and tastes. Actually, the Puccia is "only" a particular kind of bread made with Semolina Flour. These crumbless and very soft "buns" are filled with... whatever you want. The limit lies only in your imagination and the ingredients you have on hand at the moment. Whether you are a die-hard carnivore or a convinced vegetarian, you will certainly not be disappointed with the results. Just to give you an idea, in the places dear to the Lecce "movida", there are counters with countless trays from which customers can choose their favorite fillings, mixing them in endless combinations. Between you and me: temptation to put them all together in the Puccia at those times is really strong!

Difficulty: Medium - Preparation: Medium - Cost: Content

What You Need (For 6 people):

For the Main Dough
- 00 flour: 1,1 lb
- 1 lb durum wheat semolina.
- 2 Boiled Potatoes (mashed or mashed).
- Salt (about 3 tablespoons).
- Water – 20,3 oz
- Honey - 2 tablespoons.

For the Yeast Dough
- 2,64 oz durum wheat semolina.
- 2,64 of 00 flour.
- 0,24 of Brewer's Yeast (more or less a third of the classic 0,7 oz loaf).
- Sugar - 1 teaspoon.
- Water 2,5 oz

How to Prepare:

- First prepare the Yeast Dough by heating the Water and pouring in both the flours, Yeast and Sugar. Mix well and knead.

- Let the Yeast Dough rest well covered and in a warm place for a couple of hours, until it reaches twice its initial volume.

- Now add all the other ingredients to the Yeast Dough, pouring in the warm Water little by little (adjust to get a fairly firm and elastic consistency) and knead well for at least 10 to 15 minutes. The final dough should not be sticky.

- Once the dough is ready, divide it into balls that you will knead and crush a little to form individual Pucce (the ideal diameter is about 5,9 in but some people prefer them even wider, up to 7,9 in). Flour them one by one with Semolina Flour. Sprinkle a large baking sheet with the same Flour and arrange the Pucce inside.

- Bake the Pucce in the oven at 440 °F for a good half hour, checking that the surface takes on a nice even browning.

- Let them cool a bit and when they become warm... "unleash Hell" (quote).

I Frisedd' - AKA the Pugliese "Friselle" or "Frise"

And here they are! The paradigm of the "poor" and simple cuisine. What else could be said about this kind of "bread" made with a bit of Flour, Water, Yeast and Salt? It was popular imagination and inventiveness that, through the idea of biscuit-making, "gave shape" to these few ingredients and turned them into an element that can be used as a base for appetizers, side dishes and one-dish meals. And they keep for a long time, too! Which also goes well with the hectic pace of modern life: they are already there ready and in a few minutes you can set up a tasty and nutritious dish, without even turning on a stove!

Difficulty: Medium - Preparation: Long - Cost: Moderate

What You Need (For 20 Friselle)
- Remilled durum wheat semolina – 1 lb
- 00 flour – 1,45 lb
- 1 Loaf of Beer Yeast (about 7 oz) - Alternatively, 2 teaspoons of the one in a sachet.
- Salt – 0,7 oz
- Water – 20,3 oz

How to Prepare:
- Mix 7 oz of Semolina and 7 oz of Flour, then put them in a bowl, then add about 7 oz of warm water and the Yeast. Mix until everything is well blended.
- Cover this resulting soft dough with a cloth and let it rest in a warm, dry place for a couple of hours. By the end of the rising time it will have taken on a boiling appearance.
- At this point, add the rest of the Flours and Water and start kneading for a few minutes. Add the Salt and then continue kneading until you have obtained a nice smooth and compact "Ball" of dough that you will dust with a bit of 00 Flour.
- Now let it rise again, covering the dough with a cloth, for another 2 to 3 hours, until the dough has increased three times its initial volume.
- Divide the dough into 10 equal parts and knead them to give it a round shape. With floured fingers, make a hole in the center of each loaf and enlarge it a little.

- Prepare a baking tray with baking paper and arrange the "Taralli" thus obtained side by side. Let them rest for another hour. Then, give the holes a little more widening and bake for 15 minutes at 390 °F.
- Once this first baking is completed, take the Baking Pan out of the oven and cut the Frise in half (obviously, so as to form two and not through the hole).
- Bring the oven to 320 - 340 °F and bake the Friselle again for half an hour, until they have become nicely browned and crispy.
- Remove them from the oven and let them cool.

At this point the Friselle are ready to be used, in the way you prefer. The "classic" one found on all Apulian tables is with Tomatoes.

You soak the Frise with warm water - little by little without exaggerating, otherwise they will "soak" too much. You cut the Tomatoes in half and rub a couple of them on the Frise squeezing them a little. Then, garnish with the remaining Tomatoes, Extra Virgin Olive Oil (EVO), a pinch of Salt and a sprinkling of Oregano.

The variations, however, are endless and depend only on your imagination... from Eggplant or Mushrooms in oil, to grilled vegetables, Tuna, Olives and the Flavors you prefer. Experiment as much as you like because they... the Friselle, will certainly not betray you.

First Courses

Orecchiette and Turnip Greens - (I Strasc'net')

The prototype of the "Poor" Cuisine where with a little Flour (or Semolina) and Water, our ancestors gave free rein to their imagination, creating endless varieties of pasta, tasty and flavorful, with what little they had available. Orecchiette can be prepared in many ways, but they are universally known for their "pairing" with Turnip Greens, another cheap and readily available ingredient. Also different were the ways of preparing them: each housewife had her own procedures and secrets. The one I propose here is precisely the "Basic" recipe that uses only Remilled Semolina and Water.

Difficulty: Medium - Preparation: Medium - Cost: Moderate

What You Need (For 4 people):

For the Orecchiette:
   - 10,6 oz Semolina Rimacinata di Grano duro flour
   - 7 oz hot (not boiling) water

For the Condiment:
   - 3,3 lb Turnip Greens
   - Extra Virgin Olive Oil (EVO)
   - Anchovies in oil
   - Salt
   - Garlic (a couple of cloves)

How to Prepare:
   - In an appropriate container mix the Semolina with the Water, trying to blend the mixture as much as possible.
   - Then start kneading by hand on the work surface. You should get a nice compact, non-sticky dough. Then adjust by adding a bit more Water or Flour as needed. It will take at least 10 to 15 minutes to reach an optimal result.
   - Now cut out "strings" of dough that you will work with your hands to give it an even shape along the entire length. Using a knife, divide the strings into many small pieces (a bit like you do for Gnocchi). And now comes the best part (I strongly recommend you look for

a Video tutorial on the Web) because the characteristic of the Strasc'net' lies precisely in their shape, given by the right movement of the knife (some use a fork) that, pressing on the ball of dough, moves "strascinando" the same giving it precisely the characteristic shape.

- The Orecchiette should be placed on a board (there is no Apulian housewife who does not have a special wooden board) dusted with Semolina Flour and left to rest for a few hours.

- While the Orecchiette are resting, wash and clean the Turnip Greens. Then separate the leaves and stems. You will use only the leaves.

- Now prepare a sauté with the Evo Oil, Garlic, 2 or 3 anchovies in oil and possibly, a little ground Chili Pepper. When the garlic is golden brown, turn it off and keep aside while warm.

- Meanwhile, in a nice large pot you will have brought the water for the pasta to a boil and salted it. Then pour in the Cime di Rapa and cook for at least 5 to 6 minutes.

- Now add the Orecchiette, which, poured directly into the cooking water of the Turnip tops, will best absorb the flavor. The cooking time varies (depending on the consistency you have given the pasta) between 3 and 5 minutes. Keep an eye on them and drain them when they are „al dente" with a skimmer.

- Now drain the turnip greens and pour them into the stir-fry, with a little cooking water if necessary. Let them sit for a couple of minutes on low heat until everything blends well. Then add the Orecchiette as well and let it go for another couple of minutes.

- That's it, now everything is ready to plate and serve at the table with the ever-present drizzle of EVO oil to further flavor this delicacy.

Orecchiette Cozze e Fagioli

This decidedly tasty dish is a variation of the equally tasty one prepared with Cavatelli. In both cases, we have the essence of Puglia condensed into one dish: from the sea to the more inland areas, each brings its own fruits, which blend perfectly with one another.

Difficulty: Easy - Preparation: Medium - Cost: Moderate

What You Need (For 4 people):
- 14 oz of Orecchiette
- 10,6 oz of Cannellini beans
- 3,3 to 4,5 lb of Mussels
- 12 Tomatoes (Col Pizzo or Ciliegini)
- Garlic - A couple of cloves
- Extra Virgin Olive Oil (EVO)
- Ground Pepper
- Parsley

How to Prepare:
- For the preparation of Orecchiette I refer you to the recipe with Turnip Greens, but you can also use bought ones.
- As usual, clean the Mussels well and then put them in a pot, cover with a lid and leave them a few minutes on the stove until all the shells have opened.
- Strain the cooking liquid and keep it aside. Then remove about half of the mussels from their shells and place them in a bowl.
- Now prepare a frying pan with a little EVO oil and a clove of garlic. Let it brown and then add the tomatoes that you have already washed and cut in half.
- After 4 to 5 minutes, pour the Cannellini Beans (canned ones are fine too) into the pan.
- After another 5 minutes, it is now the turn of the Mussels (both those with the shell still on and those without), which you will add to the pan along with the filtered water. Let it simmer while you cook the Orecchiette.
- In the meantime, you will have brought a pot with water to a boil and can pour in the orecchiette. The cooking time varies from 3 to 5 minutes.

- Drain the Orecchiette al dente with a skimmer and place them in the pan with everything else. Mix well and if necessary, add a little cooking water.
- Now you can serve at the table, with a sprinkling of finely chopped Parsley and a little ground Black Pepper.

Orecchiette (or Cavatelli) with Burrata and Sundried Tomatoes in Oil

A very easy (and very quick, if you use ready-made pasta) first course to prepare, but no less tasty than the others I propose. An alternative to Orecchiette are the equally typical Cavatelli.

Difficulty: Easy - Preparation: Quick - Cost: Moderate

What You Need (For 4 people):
- 1 Burrata Pugliese (about 12.5 oz)
- 0.9 lb of Orecchiette or Cavatelli pasta
- 6 to 8 sun-dried tomatoes in oil

How to Prepare:
- Cut the Tomatoes into pieces and blend most of them with a homogenizer.
- Put the water for cooking in a pot, bring it to a boil and add salt. Pour in the Orecchiette (or Cavatelli). After 3 to 5 minutes they should be ready „al dente". Drain them with a skimmer and place them in a large salad bowl. Now open the Burrata, breaking it into several pieces, directly on top of the Orecchiette and add the blended tomatoes. Mix everything together well.
- Prepare the plates and spread the remaining chunks of Tomatoes on top.
- Well...didn't I say it was quick?

Pasta with Tomatoes, Eggplant and Black Olives

Here is another one of those simple pasta dishes made with the fruits of the earth and therefore, linked to a centuries-old tradition. Again, you can use your choice of either Orecchiette, Cavatelli, Troccoli or Minchiareddi. In any case, the result will always be "special."

Difficulty: Easy - Preparation: Quick - Cost: Moderate

What You Need (For 4 people):
  - 0.9 lb of ready-made Orecchiette (or other typical pasta)
  - 3 Eggplants, not too big
  - About ten cherry tomatoes (Col Pizzo or Ciliegini)
  - 1 Onion (Here I propose a "treat" - if you can find them, use Acquaviva Onions. Just to give you an idea, they are comparable to the very famous Tropea Onions and are also great in the oven)
  - 5.5 oz pitted Black Olives
  - Extra Virgin Olive Oil (EVO)
  - Parsley
  - Ground pepper
  - Salt
  - "Cacioricotta" cheese. Alternatively, you can use the Parmiggiano Reggiano DOP

How to Prepare:
  - First, you will need to wash and clean the Eggplants. Then cut them into small pieces and put them to drain after sprinkling them with salt, with a weight on top so that they remove excess water. Let them rest for half an hour.
  - Wash and cut (into 2 or 4 parts) the Cherry Tomatoes. Cut the Onion into very thin slices and cut half of the Olives into pieces as well.
  - Brown the Onion in a frying pan with a drizzle of EVO Oil and when it is golden brown add the Olives and Eggplant.
  - After a few minutes add the Cherry Tomatoes as well. Adjust the salt and pepper and add a half glass of water and let everything stew on low heat for about twenty minutes, until the Eggplants have reached the right softness.

- Meanwhile, you will have boiled water and once the "sauce" is ready you can pour in the pasta. After 3 to 5 minutes it should be al dente and then you can drain it with a skimmer and pour it into the pan. A couple of minutes on high heat, stirring well, will be enough.

- Sprinkle everything with very finely chopped Parsley (but why not try Oregano instead?) and serve at the table. And here the applause is sure to go off!

Troccoli alla Foggiana

Here is another type of pasta that in Apulia, and especially in the Foggia area, comes from a long tradition. Let us not forget that it is precisely in the province of Foggia that the famous Tavoliere delle Puglie, or the "Granary of Italy," extends. The main peculiarity of Troccoli is that they are worked with a special bronze rolling pin called "Trucculature." We can also use a more common one made of grooved wood.

In the recipe that I am proposing here, the essence of the different Apulian souls is brought together: the flavors and aromas of the sea combine with those of the land, always maintaining that "Poverty" and that simplicity of the ingredients that compose it. Of course, this type of Pasta, also goes well with many other ingredients, whether vegetable, meat or fish.

Difficulty: Medium - Preparation: Medium - Cost: Moderate

What You Need (For 4 people):

For the Troccoli
- Semolina di Grano Duro Rimacinata – 0.9 lb
- Extra Virgin Olive Oil (EVO)
- 2 Small Eggs
- Salt

For the Dressing
- Dried Pugliese Tomatoes – 3.5 oz
- Salted Anchovies – 1.8 oz (for a more delicate flavor you can use those in oil)
- Extra Virgin Olive Oil (EVO)
- Garlic - 1 clove
- 1 dried red pepper.
- Dry bread
- Salt

How to Prepare:

- First prepare the Troccoli. Then arrange the Semolina Flour in the shape of a truncated cone on the work surface. In the center add the Eggs, two tablespoons of EVO Oil, half a glass of warm Water and a pinch of Salt.

- Mix everything together with the help of a spoon or fork and then knead the dough by hand until it becomes smooth and firm.

- Divide the resulting dough into two/three equal parts and then roll them out with a common rolling pin. Be careful not to make the sheet too thin, as the Troccoli must have a certain consistency.

- Now pass the Trucculature over the sheets, thus obtaining the shape of the individual Troccoli, which you will then gently divide with floured fingers. Place them on a tray to rest for a while while you get busy preparing the sauce.

- In fact, you will have already soaked the Dried Tomatoes in a bowl of warm water. Now dry them and cut them into small pieces or rather thin slices.

- Rinse the Anchovies to remove excess salt, open them in two and remove both the bone and the tail, then chop them with a knife.

- Prepare a frying pan with a little Evo oil and, when hot, pour in the Tomatoes, Anchovies, Garlic and Chili (also chopped). After a couple of minutes, remove this pan from the heat.

- Crumble the Stale Bread by removing the crust and put it to brown, with a layer of EVO Oil in a separate pan.

- Now boil the Troccoli in a pot of salted water. After a few minutes, no more than 4 or 5, drain them well „al dente".

- Turn the heat back on under the pan with the Tomatoes and add the freshly drained Troccoli. Mix everything together and then pour them into a large soup pot.

- At the end, cover everything with the browned Breadcrumbs, mix well and serve.
- Well...I almost envy you!

Minchiaredd' e Pulupitt' (Minchiareddi and Meatballs) with Tomato Sauce

With this recipe you will kill "two birds with one stone," since you will prepare both the first and second course. In fact, Minchiareddi (another traditional pasta, especially from Salento) will be dressed with the sauce made from tasty meatballs. Unlike other specialties such as Orecchiette, Troccoli etc., Minchiareddi are distinguished by the use of Barley Flour.

Difficulty: Medium - Preparation: Medium - Cost: Moderate

What is needed (For 6 people):

For the Dough
- Barley flour - 1.3 lb
- Wheat flour - 1.3 lb
- Salt
- Water

For the Meatballs, Sauce and Dressing
- Ground Veal – 1.1 lb
- 2 Eggs
- Peeled tomatoes or tomato sauce – 1.8 lb
- Dry bread (crumbs)
- Extra Virgin Olive Oil (EVO)
- 2 Medium Eggs
- Milk – 3.4 oz
- 2 Small Onions
- Dry white wine - 1 glass
- Salt
- Grated aged Cacioricotta cheese (alternatively, Parmiggiano Reggiano DOP or Pecorino)

How to Prepare:

- Combine the two flours on the work surface and mix well. Then add a little warm water and a pinch of Salt. Knead the dough for a long time until you get a ball, nice, homogeneous and elastic. Let it rest for half an hour.

- Now divide the dough into small pieces and work them individually into strings. Each of these then divide them in turn into pieces (puddings) about 2 in long and 0.2 in thick.

- At this point, to make the Minchiareddi, tradition dictates that you use an Iron called a "Cavaturu," but if you cannot find one, you can try using one of those used for knitting, not too large in diameter and about 1 ft long. Now insert the iron in the middle of a gut and then, with a rather quick movement, rotate the iron first toward you and then in the opposite direction. Again I recommend that you look for a Tutorial on the Web to get a good understanding of the dexterity of this operation.

- Once you have prepared the Minchiareddi, let them rest on top of a tray while you devote yourself to preparing the Meatballs al Sugo.

- In a tureen combine the Mince, Eggs, Dry Bread soaked in warm water and then well squeezed, Milk and Salt to taste (but do not overdo it). Mix everything well with the help of a fork. Then, with your hands, form round balls (but slightly flattened ones are fine) of 1.6 to 2 in diameter.

- Slice the Onions and brown them in a large pan along with a little EVO Oil.

- Now add the meatballs and brown them, turning them several times. Be careful, especially at first, not to break them during the operation. When they are browned, deglaze with White Wine and add the Sauce or Pelati (made into pieces). Adjust the Salt if necessary and let it cook (with the lid on) for at least half an hour over low heat, stirring occasionally, until the Sauce has taken on a nice thick consistency. Then if you like the Sugo slower, add a tiny bit of water or let it cook a little less.

- When the Sugo is ready you can "throw the pasta" into the salted water that you will have brought to a boil in the meantime. The Minchiaredd' will be ready in a few minutes.

- Drain and serve, covering the pasta with some of the Meatball Sauce. Sprinkle with plenty of grated cheese.

As we have seen, in this way we have both the first and second course of our "hearty" meal ready, but there is also the possibility of a variation. Instead of the classic large meatballs, we can prepare many smaller meatballs (about 1 cm in diameter) and season the

Minchiareddi with the combination of the Sauce and the Meatballs, to form a single and very tasty dish.

Orecchiette with Green Beans and Cacioricotta Cheese

Here is another simple yet flavorful dish made with a few easy-to-find ingredients. Instead of Orecchiette you can use any of the traditional pastas we have already seen in other recipes: from Troccoli to Minchiareddi to Cavatelli. The result is assured anyway.

Difficulty: Easy - Preparation: Quick - Cost: Moderate

What You Need (For 4 people):
  - Fresh Pasta (see above) – 1.1 lb
  - Peeled Tomatoes - 1.1 lb
  - Tomato Sauce – 0.45 lb
  - Fresh Green Beans - 1.1 lb
  - Extra Virgin Olive Oil (EVO)
  - Grated aged Cacioricotta cheese – 1.8 oz
  - 1 Medium Onion
  - Ground Pepper
  - Salt

How to Prepare:
  - After cleaning the Green Beans well and removing their tips, boil them in salted water for about ten minutes.
  - Prepare a sauté with the finely chopped Onion and EVO Oil. When the Onion is golden brown add the boiled Green Beans. After a few minutes also add the Pelati, which you will have already coarsely chopped. If the sauce thickens too much for your taste, use some of the Tomato Sauce to thin it out. Add a little Salt and leave to simmer.
  - Meanwhile, boil salted water for the pasta. Using fresh Pasta this will be ready in a few minutes and you will need to drain it al dente.
  - Add the drained pasta to the pan (or saucepan) with the sauce and stir well for a few minutes over low heat.
  - Now serve on a plate and sprinkle with plenty of Cacioricotta and a pinch of Pepper.

Pasta with Ricotta Forte

Ricotta Forte (also known as Squant' which means Melted) is a creamy and characteristic cheese with a distinctive flavor (a little spicy and bitter) much loved by Apulians. It is used in several ways and the most "famous" ones are precisely Pasta with Ricotta Squant' and the filling of Panzerotti. In the case of our Pasta (a choice of Orecchiette, Cavatelli or so) the ease and speed of preparation is almost... embarrassing.

Difficulty: Easy - Preparation: Quick - Cost: Moderate

What is needed (per Person):

- 4.3 per person of Fresh Pasta (Orecchiette, Cavatelli, Minchiareddi, Troccoli)
- 7 oz of Tomato Sauce (or passata)
- 1 Tablespoon of Ricotta Squant'
- Extra Virgin Olive Oil (EVO)
- 1 Leaf of Basil
- ¼ Onion
- Salt

How to Prepare:

- Prepare a sauté with thinly sliced Onion with a mandoline, chopped Basil, EVO Oil and a little Salt.
- When the Onion is golden brown, add the Tomato Sauce. Let it cook for a few minutes.
- Add the Ricotta Forte to the sauce, stir well and turn off the heat after a couple of minutes. The sauce is ready!
- Boil salted water for the Pasta, which you will then drain when it is al dente (3 - 5 minutes of cooking time).
- Season the Pasta with the Sugo while still hot and serve at the table.

Pasta coi Cicer' (Chickpeas)

A specialty widespread throughout Puglia, but particularly in Salento, where Trya (a kind of handmade noodle) is used as the pasta. You, however, can prepare it with any of the pastas we have seen so far. For this reason, in the description I will only talk about the "general" preparation of the dish. I warn you that you will have to use many rare and very expensive elements... and of course, I'm kidding!

Difficulty: Easy - Preparation: Long - Cost: Content

What You Need (For 4 people):

- Prepare about 14 oz of fresh pasta dough and make Cavatelli or Minchiareddi (as per previous recipes) using 10.5 oz of it. Keep aside the other 3.5 oz of pasta
- Dried Chickpeas – 1.8 lb
- Extra Virgin Olive Oil (EVO)
- Garlic - 2 or 3 cloves
- Celery - 2 or 3 stalks
- 2 medium onions
- 2 Peeled Tomatoes
- Parsley (optional)
- Sodium bicarbonate powder
- Salt

How to Prepare:

- The chickpeas should be soaked as early as the night before to soften them. To improve and speed up the process (otherwise sometimes a whole night may not be enough) add a teaspoon of Sodium Bicarbonate.
- The next morning, when preparing lunch (n.b. well in advance), rinse and drain them thoroughly.
- Place the Chickpeas in a large saucepan (the ideal one would be earthenware) along with the peeled Garlic, the Celery stalks, the Onions cut into 4 pieces each and the Coarsely chopped Peeled tomatoes.
- Pour water (not cold) into the saucepan until it almost covers everything and add the Salt, half a teaspoon of Sodium Bicarbonate, plenty of Extra Virgin Olive Oil (EVO) and

possibly, some chopped Parsley. Cook for at least a couple of hours (but a little longer certainly doesn't hurt) on low heat. A foam will form on the surface that you will have to remove from time to time.

- When the cooking is done, you can remove the Celery and Garlic from the mixture.
- Now cut the Pasta you had kept aside into small pieces 5 to 10 cm long to form small cylinders and fry them with a little EVO Oil.
- In the meantime, you will have brought the Salted Water to a boil to cook the Pasta. Drain the Pasta al dente (in 3 - 5 minutes it is usually ready) and prepare the dishes by combining the Pasta with the preparation with the Chickpeas.
- Complete by adding a few pieces of Fried Pasta to each one.
- Result-guaranteed!

Cavatelli with Cardoncelli Mushrooms (and Sausage)

Very widespread in the region - so much so that they have been certified PAT - Prodotto Agroalimentare Tradizionale Italiano (Traditional Italian Food Product) - by Mipaaf - Cardoncelli Mushrooms[3] are for this reason present in various dishes of Apulian Tradition. One of these is Pasta with Cardoncelli and Sausage (in this case I mean the Typical one, long and narrow, called Cervellata - See dedicated recipe). Orecchiette, Cavatelli or Minchiareddi are fine for preparing this quick and tasty first course.

Difficulty: Easy - Preparation: Quick - Cost: Moderate

What You Need (For 4 people):
- Cavatelli – 1.1 lb
- Cervellata (Pork or Mixed) – 0.9lb
- Cardoncelli – 0.8 lb
- 7 oz of Tomato Sauce
- 1 Onion
- Garlic (1 or 2 cloves)
- Extra Virgin Olive Oil (EVO)
- Dry white wine
- Grated aged Cacioricotta cheese – 1.8 oz
- Ground pepper (or chili pepper)
- Salt

How to Prepare:
- Clean and wash the Mushrooms well, then cut them into medium-thick (0.11 to 0.2 in) slices.
- Peel the Cervellata and crumble it into a bowl.
- Chop the Onion and sauté in a large frying pan with a little EVO Oil, the peeled Garlic and a pinch of Pepper (alternatively, chopped dried Chili).
- When the Onion is wilted, pour the Sausage into the sauté and brown it well, stirring often.

- At this point, deglaze it with a little White Wine and let the alcohol evaporate. Remove the Garlic.

- Add the Cardoncelli Mushrooms and lower the heat under the pan a little. After a few minutes pour in the Tomato Sauce and if necessary, dilute the sauce with a little water.

- Let it simmer for about a quarter of an hour. Meanwhile put the salted water to boil to cook the Pasta.

- As you know by now by heart, drain the Pasta when it is al dente (3 - 5 minutes).

- Now toss the Pasta back into the pan and stir well over low heat for a couple of minutes.

- Serve on plates with a sprinkling of grated Cacioricotta cheese.

Pasta with Urchins

This is surely another of the most delicious specialties of Puglia. In fact, it is easy to find urchins in many of the region's endless coastal locations. After Mussels, they are among the most sought-after and appreciated seafood. Delicious eaten raw, they are also great for dressing pasta: you will enjoy all the flavor and scent of the sea in one dish. The only problem is that not all months are ideal for fishing, and so it is preferable to enjoy them in the winter months or early spring, so as to find their "flesh" at its peak development.

Difficulty: Easy - Preparation: Quick - Cost: Moderate

What You Need (For 4 people):
- Sea urchins: 20 to 25 per person
- Linguine or Spaghetti: 11.2 oz
- Extra Virgin Olive Oil (EVO)
- Garlic 1 clove
- Salt
- Ground pepper or crushed dried chili pepper
- Parsley

How to Prepare:
- First, be careful not to hurt yourself handling the urchins. To open them, equip yourself with special gloves and a hedgehog cutter (or sharp scissors. I strongly recommend watching some Tutorials on the Net.
- Once you have washed and then opened the urchins, use a teaspoon to scrape out the pulp and place it in a cup. In another cup instead, drain the liquid you will find inside.
- Strain the liquid through a fine-mesh strainer or gauze.
- Now prepare a pan with a bit of EVO oil, some of the strained liquid, the peeled garlic clove and the finely chopped Parsley.
- Boil the salted water for the pasta and then drain the latter when it is al dente.
- Add the pasta to the sauté and let it stir over low heat, adding the rest of the strained liquid. Only at the last (and for no more than a minute) add the urchin flesh.
- Now you can serve on a plate, sprinkling with pepper or chili to taste. The Sea is ready on the table!

Orecchiette with Sardines and Turnip Greens

From what I've written so far, I think by now you are beginning to have the "vague suspicion" that here in Puglia, it is not as if we waste too much time on expensive dishes and the most difficult (or inconstant) ingredients to find. Hence the many ways of using Mussels, which far outweigh the use of other seafood. In fact, for those who still don't know, there would not even be a need for recipes for Mussels... because the "true" DOC Apulian, Mussels eat them strictly raw!

Same thing also applies to Blue Fish. The "TRUE" Traditional recipes in fact are mainly based on the latter (Anchovies and Sardines in particular). They are very common fish in our seas, easily (at least compared to others) caught in abundance and very cheap (especially in the past... when they were the fish of the poors who, in turn, were the vast majority of the population). These reasons made them (unintentionally, thanks to their rich Omega 3 content) also real cornerstones in the so-called "Mediterranean Diet," which was later proven to be not only delicious and cheap, but also healthy.

Difficulty: Easy - Preparation: Medium - Cost: Moderate

What You Need (For 4 people):
- Orecchiette (any of the types of homemade pasta we talked about will do) – 1.1 lb
- Turnip greens – 2.2 lb
- Fresh sardines – 0.9 lb
- Garlic (a couple of cloves)
- Red pepper
- Extra Virgin Olive Oil (EVO)
- A few dried tomatoes in oil
- Salt

How to Prepare:

- First you will need to clean the sardines thoroughly (unless the fishmonger has already done so), removing both the innards, the inner bone and the fins/tails. In any case, then wash them thoroughly under running water and dry them with a clean cloth

- Now heat some EVO Oil in a pan, along with the garlic (peeled) and the chili pepper in pieces. When it is hot, add the Sardines as well. When their flesh has turned white (it is pink at first), add the chopped Tomatoes. Now remove the pan from the heat.

- Separately, you will have already boiled the Turnip Greens in salted water for 10 to 15 minutes (see recipe for Orecchiette with Turnip Greens). When they are ready, add them to the pan with the Sardines.

- Now you can boil the salted water to cook the pasta. As you know by now by heart, it will only take 3 to 5 minutes to be able to drain it al dente.

- Add the Pasta to the saucepan with the Sardines and vegetables and stir everything well over low heat.

- Plate and serve on the table piping hot.

Vegetable and Meatless Dishes

The Stuffed Eggplants (I Marangèll' Chièn')

This is my favorite recipe ever! And I have a hard time placing it in a specific section of this book. Is it a main course? Is it a side dish? Is it a very tasty appetizer? Well, I don't care! What matters is that someone invented it. And that my Aunt Barbara (followed by her daughter Maria) brought this recipe to perfection!

Difficulty: Easy - Preparation: Medium - Cost: Moderate

What You Need (For 4 people):

 - 4 Eggplants - Ideal ones are medium-sized (about 6 x 4 in) and neither too round nor too elongated in shape. Of course, it is preferable to prepare this dish during the summer, when the eggplants themselves are more flavorful and "sweet."
 - 7 oz dry bread.
 - 3 Eggs
 - 10.6 oz Tomato Sauce
 - Salted Capers
 - Basil
 - 1.8 oz Grated Pecorino Cheese (alternatively you can use Parmggiano Reggiano DOP or Cacioricotta)
 - Extra Virgin Olive Oil (EVO)
 - Oregano (I recommend that you also experiment with Basil and Parsley and see which suits your taste best)
 - Salt

How to Prepare:

 - First you will need to wash the Eggplants and cut them in half, lengthwise. Basically, they should take the shape of a small boat. Cover them with salt and a good weight on top. Leave them like this overnight, so that they expel excess water.
 - In a frying pan with Olio Evo and a clove of garlic, fry the eggplant halves, turning them often, until you see that they soften and wrinkle.
 - Let them cool a bit so that you can then handle them. At this point, scoop out the inner pulp, leaving only a narrow outer edge. put the pulp in a bowl and keep the rest aside.

- Now add the Eggs, the Tomato Sauce, the dry Bread that you will have soaked in warm water in the meantime, and the Pecorino cheese. Mix everything together until the mixture is smooth.

- Then add the Capers (after leaving them for a while in a cup of warm water to remove excess salt and drained well) and a sprinkling of Oregano. Stir well again. (A secret: Be wary of anyone who doesn't put Capers in it).

- With the resulting mixture, now fill the eggplants you had "hollowed out" earlier. Then arrange them in a well-oiled baking dish (better perhaps to use baking paper, so we avoid problems of... sticking). A drizzle of Olio Evo will complete the preparation.

- All that remains is to put in the oven (preheated to about 390 °F) for 25 to 30 minutes.

- Once finished cooking, remove the pan and let it cool to room temperature. In fact, Stuffed Eggplants are at their best when they are not warm. At least to my taste! You can also store them in the refrigerator for a day and you will see that they have not lost their taste -- quite the contrary.

Puglia Style Eggplant Parmigiana

Well, Eggplant Parmigiana is a practically universal dish of Mediterranean Cuisine, and practically every region (or country bordering the Mare Nostrum) has its own personal interpretation. What differentiates one from the other, however, is not so much the use of a component or not, but the quality of the products that are used. And here, Puglia has nothing to envy anyone. In fact, the basic ingredients (Eggplant, Tomatoes, EVO Oil) are among the best that can be found in the entire Mediterranean area.

Difficulty: Easy - Preparation: Medium - Cost: Moderate

What You Need (For 4 people):
  - 2.2 lb Eggplant
  - 1.3 lb Tomato puree or sauce
  - 5.3 oz grated Cacioricotta cheese (Alternatively, Parmigiano Reggiano DOP or Grana Padano DOP cheese)
  - 14.1 oz of Mozzarella (Andria-type nodini is ideal)
  - Basil
  - Extra Virgin Olive Oil (EVO)
  - Salt
  - Pepper

How to Prepare:
  - Wash the eggplants and cut them into slices. Lay them in layers in a colander sprinkling each layer with coarse salt and place a weight on top. Leave them like this overnight.
  - The next day, fry the Eggplants in plenty of Oil, taking care to turn them on both sides. Drain them and lay them in a large dish on which you will have placed kitchen paper. This will remove the excess oil. Note that I, in this recipe do NOT flour or prepare a flour/egg batter to fry the Eggplants. I like them that way: au naturel!
  - Now grease a baking dish (or an oven dish) with Evo oil and begin to compose a first layer of Eggplant.
  - Pour over the layer some of the Salsa, some Mozzarella cut into small pieces and some grated Cheese. Also add a chopped leaf of Basil and if you like, a pinch of Ground Pepper.

- Continue, alternating the layers in the same way. On the last layer of Eggplant, however, put only the Tomato Sauce and a generous sprinkling of Cheese.

- Now you can bake. The average baking time is about 30 minutes at 390 °F.

- When done, let it cool down thoroughly. In my (immodest) opinion, Parmigiana should be enjoyed only when it is well "rested" and at room temperature.

Fried Lampascioni

Lampascioni are a particular species of wild onions readily available in Puglia. Their taste is very particular, because of that "touch" of bitterness that counterbalances the sweetness of its aftertaste. They are usually used in oil, but they also deserve to be enjoyed fresh, as I propose in this recipe. A simple, no-frills and inexpensive dish that well represents a tradition made of poor foods, but with great flavors.

Difficulty: Easy - Preparation: Medium - Cost: Moderate

What You Need (For 4 people):

- 1.1 lb fresh Lampascioni. If you cannot find them fresh, you can always try using those in oil, obviously skipping the first steps of preparation.
- 2 Eggs
- 3.5 oz grated Cacioricotta cheese (alternatively, use Pecorino).
- Garlic
- Flour
- Extra Virgin Olive Oil (EVO)
- Parsley
- Salt

How to Prepare:

- After cleaning and peeling (like any onion) the fresh Lampascioni, make a cross cut on each one, but do not go all the way through. Then lay them in a container with cold water for 6 to 8 hours, taking care to change the water a couple of times. This will remove any impurities and also mitigate the bitter taste.
- At the end, take the Lampascioni out of the water, drain them and dry them well.
- Prepare a mixture in a large bowl with the Eggs, Cheese, 2 to 3 tablespoons of Flour, chopped Parsley and Garlic and a pinch of salt.
- Add the Lampascioni to this bowl and turn them well inside the mixture.
- Now you can fry them in a pan (or high-sided frying pan) with hot Oil. Turn them often so they do not burn. It only takes a few minutes for them to take on a golden and crispy appearance.

- Drain them and place them on kitchen paper to absorb excess Oil. Season then with a pinch of Salt and bring to the table.

Stuffed Fried Zucchini Flowers.

A recipe as easy to prepare as it is tasty and delicious. It can also go well as an appetizer. Since we are in Puglia, for the filling we can choose between Mozzarella (nodini di Andria), Stracciatella or even Burrata itself. The result will still be assured. During the long summers in our Trullo, my father used to gather them from the Garden at dawn and within a couple of hours they were already in the pan. As fresh and tasty as it gets!

Difficulty: Easy - Preparation: Quick - Cost: Moderate

What You Need (For 4 people):
- 16 Fresh Zucchini Flowers
- 5.6 oz Mozzarella (see introduction)
- 2 Eggs
- Flour
- Anchovies in oil
- Extra Virgin Olive Oil (EVO)
- Salt

How to Prepare:
- First, remove the pistil found inside the flowers. Be careful not to ruin the "petals."
- Shred the Mozzarella (or the equivalent) in a bowl.
- Gently and without exaggeration fill each flower with the Mozzarella and a small piece of Alice in oil (herein lies the little secret). Close the opening by lightly pressing the petals together.
- In a deep dish (or bowl) put a couple of tablespoons of Flour, the Eggs (without the shells...of course) and a pinch of salt. Whisk to combine. The consistency must be quite runny. We don't have to make a Tempura, just enough to give a golden, slightly crispy coating to our flowers.
- In a pan pour plenty of Evo Oil (alternatively, you can also use Sunflower or Peanuts Oil) and put it on the stove over high heat.
- Now pass the Flowers, one at a time, into the batter and then place them in the pan to fry. Turn them regularly. As soon as the surface becomes golden and slightly crispy you can

remove them from the Oil with a skimmer. Lay them on a tray with kitchen paper so that they are dry.

- Hurry up and eat them, because like all respectable fried foods -- so hot they are at their best....

Eggplant Meatballs (Fried or Baked)

Here (again) is another easy-to-prepare second course based on the "usual" few and simple ingredients that, however, when cooked the right way, give rise to the tasty dishes of Traditional Apulian Cuisine.

Difficulty: Easy - Preparation: Quick - Cost: Moderate

What You Need (For 4 people):

- 3 Eggplants, not too large. I prefer the elongated purple ones, or the relatively small and not too globular ones I recommended already in the recipe for Stuffed Eggplant.
- 2.6 oz of breadcrumbs
- 2.6 oz of Dry Bread.
- 2 Eggs
- 2 Garlic Cloves
- 1.8 oz grated Cacioricotta cheese (Parmiggiano Reggiano DOP is fine as an alternative)
- Parsley
- Ground pepper
- Salt
- EVO oil (Sunflower or Peanuts Oil are Ok too)

How to Prepare:

- First, clean and wash the eggplants.
- Cut them into very small cubes.
- Put a frying pan with a little EVO oil and a clove of Garlic on the stove, then pour in the Eggplants and cook them until they soften.
- After browning them, mash one part of these Eggplants and leave the other intact. Let them cool completely.
- Now, in a bowl, crack open an egg, put in all the eggplant, the dry bread (after soaking it in hot water and then well squeezed), the other clove of Garlic and the Parsley (both finely chopped), the grated Cheese, a pinch of Salt and Pepper. Mix and blend the mixture well.

- With a spoon scoop out some of the mixture and with your hands, make meatballs. You can give them the shape and size you prefer. I like them a little flattened and 1.6 to 1.9 in diameter.

- Now open the other Egg in a deep dish and beat it, then coat the meatballs in both the Egg and the Breadcrumbs.

- At this point, you will have two options: if you like them fried, put them in a pan with plenty of Frying Oil and brown them well. Or, if you want a lighter version, you can bake them in the oven, at 360 °F for 15 to 20 minutes.

Breadballs (with Eggs)

This, too, is a very simple dish that can be prepared and cooked in a short time and takes me back a long time with my memory. We children loved them and literally "tortured" the various aunts to make them for us. And after all, they didn't mind settling for us with so little.

Difficulty: Easy - Preparation: Quick - Cost: Content

What You Need (For 4 people):
   - Stale bread 10.6 oz (alternatively, you can also use cassette bread or breadcrumbs)
   - 2 Eggs
   - 3.5 oz grated Cacioricotta Pugliese cheese. If you do not have it you can use Pecorino or Parmigiano Reggiano DOP
   - 3.4 oz of Milk
   - Parsley
   - Salt
   - 00 Flour

How to Prepare:
   - Let the Bread soak in the Milk, then squeeze it well.
   - Combine the Bread soaked in this way with the Eggs, Cheese, Finely chopped Parsley and Salt in a large bowl.
   - Knead everything well with your hands. The final dough should be firm but soft. If necessary, add a bit more Milk.
   - Then form patties of the shape and size you prefer and roll them in 00 Flour.
   - Now you can fry them in plenty of boiling Oil for a few minutes, turning them occasionally, until they are nice and golden.
   - Remove them from the Oil, drain them and place them on paper towels to dry.
   - Serve them nice and hot.

The Mashed Broad Beans

OK, I'm putting it here in this section -- but it could be almost anywhere. In fact, Mashed Broad Beans is a kind of base/side dish for one-dish meals, but there is nothing to stop it from being eaten as an appetizer, first course or even second course. What varies are the quantities and the "things" we put next to it. In any case, this is another cornerstone of Apulian Cuisine and a further confirmation (was there still a need?) of how, with very poor elements it is possible - by working them, cooking them and combining them appropriately - to give life to recipes of extraordinary taste. The most "typical" version is with Chicory (boiled or repassed) from the field, but Mashed Broad Beans can be accompanied by practically any vegetable. Or even, replace the "classic" Mashed Potatoes as a side dish for meat dishes.

Again, I'll let you in on a little family secret -- the Bread.

Difficulty: Medium - Preparation: Long - Cost: Moderate

What You Need (For 4 people):

- Dried Broad Beans – 1.1 lb
- Potatoes – 0.45 lb
- Stale bread – 3.5 oz
- Extra Virgin Olive Oil (EVO)
- Salt.

How to Prepare:

- First you will need to soak (in a pot with cold water) the dried Broad Beans for at least 3 to 4 hours, but it is best to do this the night before.
- Start with the Potatoes, peeling and slicing them, then soak them for half an hour in water.
- Boil the Broad Beans and Potatoes in a nice large pot and add water until everything is covered.
- When the water boils, remove the foam that will form on the surface with a skimmer. Add a little Salt, cover with a lid and then let it simmer for a couple of hours. Remember to stir often, otherwise Beans and Potatoes are likely to stick to the bottom.

- When cooked, drain the mixture and mash it with a vegetable mill. Meanwhile, add the stale bread that you have already soaked in warm water and then squeezed.

- Put everything back into the pot, add a good dose of Olio Evo and a little water if it seems too compact. Now let it simmer, stirring continuously (and vigorously) with the classic wooden spoon until your Puree takes on a nice creamy consistency.

- Now you can serve it on the table (it is great either warm or hot, but it is also delicious at room temperature, and the variation in serving temperature also characterizes its use as a type of dish) with the Cicorietta ripassata in pan, but also-as mentioned-with any of the many Apulian vegetables.

Eggs and Sponsali Onions (Ciambotto)

What were the ingredients that were never lacking in Apulian country life? The Tomatoes, the local Porraie Onions (Sponsali), The Extra Virgin Olive Oil (EVO), and some Eggs. Here, by combining them all together you can easily prepare, during the winter (because that's the time of year when Sponsali can be found) this great-tasting dish.

Difficulty: Easy - Preparation: Quick - Cost: Moderate

What You Need (For 4 people):
- 4 Eggs
- 5 or 6 Sponsali (if you can't find them, you can use common spring onions, which are less sweet, though). I would maybe give Acquaviva Onions a try.
- "Col Pizzo" or Ciliegini cherry tomatoes
- Altamura bread
- Parsley
- Ground pepper
- Extra Virgin Olive Oil (EVO)
- Salt

How to Prepare:
- After cleaning and thinly slicing the Onions, sauté them in a pan with a drizzle of EVO Oil.
- When the Onion starts to brown, add the finely chopped Parsley and a few chopped Tomatoes. Also add a half glass of Water and then let it simmer for about ten minutes.
- Now open the Eggs directly into the pan of Onions. Do this carefully (as with the Ox-Eye Eggs) so as not to break the Yolk. Add the Salt and possibly, a sprinkling of Pepper.
- Let cook for a few more minutes, covering with a lid. The duration depends on how you like the Eggs (more or less cooked).
- Meanwhile, on the side, prepare croutons (or crostoni, if you use whole slices) of Bread, by toasting them in a pan with a little EVO Oil.
- Serve the Eggs on plates, where you will have previously placed a few croutons or a single slice of toasted bread

Crouton Foggia-style with Provola (or Caciocavallo cheese)

This can be a great idea when you're in a hurry, but want something tasty to...munch on. Or it can be served as an appetizer, perhaps using smaller croutons.

Difficulty: Easy - Preparation: Quick - Cost: Moderate

What is needed (For each Crostino):
   - 3.2 oz Provola or Caciocavallo cheese
   - 1 Slice of Bread (if Altamura bread is better)
   - 1 Alice in oil
   - 4 or 5 Capers in Salt
   - Butter – 0.35 oz
   - Garlic - ¼ clove

How to Prepare:
   - Desalt the Capers (in a cup with warm water) and peel the Garlic.
   - Prepare a Mince by combining Capers, Garlic and Anchovies and place in a small saucepan along with the Butter. Melt the Butter, stir well and turn off the heat.
   - Place the slices of Bread on top of a well-oiled baking sheet, or lined with baking paper. Then pour some of the sauce with the melted Butter over the individual slices.
   - Cover the Bread slices with the very finely cut Provola (or Caciocavallo) cheese. Then pour in the rest of the sauce.
   - Now you can put the pan in the oven (preheated to 360 °F) and let it bake for a few minutes, until the surface of the Crostini becomes nice and golden.
   - Easy right?

Onions of Acquaviva

The red onions of *Acquaviva delle Fonti* are the Apulian "answer" to the very famous onions of *Tropea* in Calabria. Unlike the latter, however, they are more discoidal and flattened in shape, as well as more pinkish in color. The flesh has a sweetish and delicate flavor. The cultivation of this Onion (PAT certified - Prodotto Agroalimentare Tradizionale Italiano (Traditional Italian Food Product) - by Mipaaf)[3] is very limited in extent and production is rather scarce, so if you happen to find it, don't let it pass you by. Otherwise you can always look for it and order it online.

In this case, I group below two different ways to prepare them.

Grated in the Oven

Difficulty: Easy - Preparation: Medium - Cost: Low

What You Need (For 4 people):
   - 4 Acquaviva onions (about 4 inches in diameter)
   - Grated aged Cacioricotta cheese – 1.8 oz (with the usual Parmigiano Reggiano DOP or Pecorino alternatives)
   - Salted capers (about twenty)
   - Breadcrumbs – 7 oz
   - Tomato sauce – 3.5 oz
   - Extra Virgin Olive Oil (EVO)
   - Parsley
   - Salt
   - Ground Pepper

How to Prepare:
   - Wash the Onions well and remove the surface film, then cut each in half, widthwise, to form two disks. Arrange them on top of a well-oiled baking sheet (or with Oven Paper).
   - In a bowl, mix all the other ingredients (remember to desalinate the Capers by leaving them a few minutes in a small cup with cold water) together with two/three tablespoons of EVO Oil.

- Spread the resulting mixture over the 8 Onion disks, covering the entire top surface well.

- Now place the Baking Pan in the oven (which you will have heated to 360 °F) for half an hour, until the breadcrumbs are golden and crispy.

- Let them cool and serve them on the table, as an accompaniment to other dishes, but also as a stand-alone one!

Caramelized

Difficulty: Easy - Preparation: Quick - Cost: Low

What You Need (For 4 people):
- Acquaviva onions – 1.5 lb
- Brown sugar - 2 tablespoons
- Wine Vinegar – 2.3 oz
- Extra Virgin Olive Oil (EVO)
- Salt
- Ground pepper

How to Prepare:
- Clean the Onions well, peel and wash them. Then cut them into thin slices with a mandoline.

- In a large skillet, heat a little Evo Oil and a pinch of Salt. Add the Onions and after a couple of minutes, a little water as well. Let it go on a not too high heat. When the Onions are wilted, add the Vinegar and Cane Sugar and over high heat, stir everything well until the Vinegar is completely evaporated and the sugar caramelized.

- Now you can enjoy them as is, as a side dish, or use them as appetizers or snacks over a slice of bruschetta or with small toasted bread croutons.

Meat Main Courses

Braised Gnumm'riedd'

Otherwise called Gnummaridd', 'Mboti, Turcinieddi, Turcinieddhri, etc. depending on the different areas of Puglia, these are another pillar of Apulian cuisine and yet another demonstration of the parochialism pushed to the extreme that characterizes all Italian regions. The fact remains, that in this case there is little to vary, other than the name, given the extreme simplicity and reduced number of ingredients, of a cuisine that was born "poor," but is now capable of satisfying even the most demanding palates. In my memories of (too many) years ago, I still see people leaving the butcher shops of Martina Franca on Sunday evenings (yes, even on Sunday evenings) with a pot in their hands covered with a dishcloth. Inside those pots were precisely the Gnumm'riedd' (along with Agnellone and possibly Cervellata - two other "specialties" you will find described later), freshly removed from the coals. A tradition that had been lost, starting in the 1970s, but is back in vogue in the new millennium. So when you go to Puglia, pay attention if, near the entrance to the butcher shops it says somewhere "Fornello Pronto" ... and bring your pot with you!

P.s. Be careful, because they are addictive! For example, I don't eat them anymore because I once overdid them so much that I had indigestion!

Difficulty: Easy - Preparation: Quick - Cost: Moderate

What You Need (For 4 people):

- 1.8 lb of Lamb Interiora - Heart, Lungs, Liver, Peritoneum etc. - which then more or less correspond to the elements of the otherwise well-known Coratella.
- Some lemons (3-4)
- Gut and net of Lamb
- Extra Virgin Olive Oil (EVO)
- Finely chopped parsley
- Salt
- Ground pepper

How to Prepare:

- Wash the innards well and then rub them with salt (fine) and chopped lemons.
- Then cut the liver, heart and lungs into thin strips.

- Form small piles with these mixed offal. They will be about the size of a finger in length and two fingers in width.

- Sprinkle each pile with Pepper and Parsley.

- Now tie the individual piles together with the casing and netting

- At this point, you can bbq them. Alternatively, you can use a griddle (to be greased with EVO Oil) but of course ... it will not be the same.

The Bombette (small Bombs) from Martina Franca

Present throughout Apulia, they are particularly common in the "magic" triangle of the Itria Valley. So also in Locorotondo and Cisternino. They are basically stuffed "rolls," currently also very popular as "finger food." Tradition wants them grilled, but they are also excellent cooked in the oven. As always, the special feature is given, more than by the dish itself, by the quality of the local ingredients.

Difficulty: Easy - Preparation: Quick - Cost: Medium

What You Need (For 4 people):

- Thin slices of Capocollo di Maiale (Pork Neck) Martinese. Alternatively, you can also use those of any "anonymous" pork or those of veal. At least 2 per person but-let's make it 3 or 4!
- As many (thin) slices of Pancetta.
- 3.5 to 5.3 oz of Caciocavallo Pugliese cheese. The Best variety is the „Podolico" one
- Extra Virgin Olive Oil (EVO)
- Parsley
- Garlic
- Salt
- Pepper.

How to Prepare:

- Arrange the slices on the work surface and inside each one place a slice of bacon.
- On top, place small pieces of Caciocavallo cheese (do not overdo the size) and sprinkle with chopped Garlic, Parsley and Pepper.
- Roll up the slices and close them by folding the ends over so that they take on a spherical-like shape. Secure them with a toothpick.
- At this point, grease the Bombette with a little EVO Oil, sprinkle them with Salt and if you have a nice grill available...good! If not, arrange them in a well-oiled baking dish and let them bake about 20 minutes at 390 °F

- If your oven has the Grill, now turn it on for about 10 minutes at 350 F°, checking carefully that they do not burn. If not, move the baking sheet from the middle to the top to bring it closer to the hottest part.

Cervellata with Sauce

Cervellata is a particular "Luganega"-type sausage, which originates in Toritto, in the province of Bari and also boasts PAT certification - Prodotto Agroalimentare Tradizionale Italiano - from Mipaaf. Of course, we don't care about "pieces of paper," but we do care a lot about "practice." And in this case Cervellata never disappoints. Usually, It's prepared by the butcher at will: with pork, veal or mixed meat, to which any flavorings can be added (such as wild fennel-another "secret" that I will reveal) in addition to the ever-present salt and pepper. It is usually cooked in a frying pan or on the grill, but I want to offer it here in a tasty version with sauce.

Difficulty: Easy - Preparation: Quick - Cost: Medium

What You Need (For 4 people):

- 14.1 oz of Tomatoes (preferably choose between those "Col Pizzo" and the classic cherry ones)
- 1.3 lb of Cervellata
- 1 Onion
- Extra Virgin Olive Oil (EVO)
- 1 oz of Dried Mushrooms
- Basil
- Salt

How to Prepare:

- Soak the mushrooms by placing them in a container with hot water (but not too much).
- After half an hour take them out of the water and squeeze them gently in the same water. Then strain the water and keep it aside.
- Wash the Tomatoes and cut them into 4 pieces.
- Cut the Cervellata into pieces about 6 inches each.
- Pour a drizzle of EVO Oil into the pan along with the thinly sliced Onion.
- When the Onion starts to brown add both the Tomatoes, the Mushrooms and the Cervellata.
- Simmer for about twenty minutes.
- Adjust the Salt and serve on a platter.

I Vraciulidd' - (The Braciòle)

Actually, Apulian "Braciole" are tasty stuffed meat rolls. I remember that this, the first time, generated some confusion in us "city" children, because we were obviously expecting juicy bone-in steaks. However, the "disappointment" was promptly dispelled by the final result. The traditional recipe calls for Horse Meat, but Veal is also fine.

Difficulty: Easy - Preparation: Medium - Cost: Medium

What You Need (For 5 people):

- 2 Slices (at least) per person of Horse or Veal meat. Of course, adjust the amounts below if you make more than 2.
- 2.8 oz grated "Cacioricotta" cheese. (Pecorino or Parmigiano reggiano DOP the alternatives).
- Peeled Tomatoes or Tomato Sauce 2.2 lb
- 1 1/2 onions
- Garlic (3 cloves)
- Celery Leaves
- Extra Virgin Olive Oil (EVO)
- Apulian Red Wine (one glass)
- Ground Pepper
- Salt

How to Prepare:

- Preparation is fairly simple. Start by flattening the slices arranged on the work surface.
- In each one arrange two small leaves of Celery, a little Cacioricotta cheese, a thin slice of Onion, a pinch of chopped Garlic and Parsley, a pinch of Salt and a sprinkling of Pepper.
- Roll up the slice, fold in the ends and secure with a toothpick.
- Now brown, in a high-sided pan, some sliced Onion.
- At this point add the Braciole and brown them well on all sides.
- Deglaze with the Red Wine.

- Now also pour the chopped peeled tomatoes (or sauce) into the pan. Stir well and let simmer for a good hour or so. Check occasionally that the sauce does not thicken too much. If it does, add a little water.

- The long cooking in the sauce will give softness to the Braciole. The same sauce (which in fact we have dosed generously) you can use to season a tasty first course made with Orecchiette or Cavatelli.

Agnellone al Forno con i Lampascioni (Lamb in the oven with Lampascioni)

As mentioned earlier in the recipe for Gnumm'riedd', in Martina Franca, Agnellone (i.e. a lamb slaughtered when aged 6 to 10 months) is widely used, especially grilled, and has always been preferred to the classic Suckling Lamb (the so called Abbacchio); therefore, I have included it as the cornerstone of the recipe, but you can of course decide otherwise. Either way, the dish will turn out tasty and flavorful.

Difficulty: Easy - Preparation: Medium - Cost: Medium

What You Need (For 4 people):
- Agnellone Martinese – 3.3 lb
- Apulian Lampascioni – 1.1 lb
- 4 Large Potatoes
- 3 Onions
- Extra Virgin Olive Oil (EVO)
- Grated Cacioricotta cheese - (as an alternative, use Pecorino cheese)
- A few cloves of Garlic
- 5 - 6 "Col Pizzo" or Ciliegini tomatoes
- Parsley
- Celery
- Ground Pepper
- Salt
- Dried chili pepper (Optional)

How to Prepare:
- After cleaning and peeling (like any onion) the fresh Lampascioni, cut them into 4 parts. Then lay them in a container with cold water for 6 to 8 hours, taking care to change the water a couple of times. This will remove any impurities and also mitigate the bitter taste. Alternatively, you can use Lampascioni preserved in oil.
- Wash and dry well the Lamb meat made into pieces.
- Cut the Potatoes, Onions and Lampascioni into pieces.

- Prepare a mince with the Parsley, I Pomodorini, Celery and Garlic. Also add Salt and Pepper.

- Oil a large baking dish (or Pyrex dish) and arrange the meat and vegetable pieces inside. Cover everything with the Chop (possibly add some Chili too) and sprinkle with plenty of grated Cacioricotta cheese.

- Before baking, pour a generous amount of EVO Oil on the surface.

- Bake at 320 to 340 °F for about two hours.

The Chicken "Cusutu 'Nculu" - AKA, Stuffed Chicken.

Stuffed Chicken is certainly not exclusive to Apulian Cuisine, but it is nevertheless a traditional dish of it, especially in Salento. Much loved on holydays. The particular "name" of this recipe was also brought to the fore by a well-known Apulian comedian, which helped spread its popularity beyond the regional borders. In fact, "Cusutu 'Nculu" means „Sewn in the butt" :-)

Difficulty: Easy - Preparation: Medium - Cost: Medium

What You Need (For 4 people):
- Of course, you need a nice whole Chicken with its innards.
- 5.3 oz pork belly cut into thin slices
- Extra Virgin Olive Oil (EVO)
- 1 Onion
- Garlic (2-3 cloves)
- A couple of dried chilies
- Salt
- Ground Pepper
- Kitchen Twine

How to Prepare:
- First, you will need to remove the legs, eviscerate the Chicken and then knife up the innards, which you will keep aside in a bowl. Watch out for the Gricile (or Grecile/Ventriglio) which must be opened, cleaned and washed thoroughly before chopping.
- Wash the Chicken thoroughly both externally and internally. Burn on the stove any remnants of feathers/feathers.
- Now prepare a mince with the Bacon, Garlic, Onion and Chilies.
- Combine the mince with the entrails, add the EVO Oil, salt and a sprinkling of Ground Pepper. Mix the mixture well until it is as smooth as possible.
- Now fill the inside of the chicken with this mixture and sew the openings with Twine. Also tie the thighs tightly to the body.

- Oil a baking sheet (or an oven dish) and place the Chicken inside. Bake at 390 °F for about an hour, taking care to turn the Chicken occasionally on all its sides.
- When it is cooked, let it cool a little bit and then serve on the table. As a side dish, classic baked potatoes are the "standard" but, as always, it also goes to personal taste. I suggest you try Acquaviva delle Fonti Onions (you will find recipes in the Vegetable Dishes section) and you will see that you will not be disappointed.

Fish Main Courses

Octopus in Pignatta

Even in the case of Fish dishes, the Tradition of this land prefers simple and easily available ingredients. And what could be simpler than a tasty Octopus, which can be caught almost anywhere along the region's extensive coastline? How many times, in the summer at the beach, have I seen young and old alike turn into "hunters" armed with a simple little bow? How many times then, have I seen the same ones "soften" the octopuses thus caught by vigorously banging them on the rocks? These are images anyone can see, as widespread as they are in our Apulia region. So, once caught, how do we cook this octopus? With this recipe, as simple as it is mouthwatering.

Difficulty: Easy - Preparation: Medium - Cost: Content

What You Need (For 4 people):
  - Octopus 1.8 to 2.6 lb
  - 0.9 lb Potatoes
  - Extra Virgin Olive Oil (EVO)
  - Dry white wine
  - Onion
  - Garlic
  - Parsley
  - Ground Pepper
  - Salt

How to Prepare:
  - Clean and wash the Octopus thoroughly, then cut it into not very large pieces.
  - Place the Octopus thus cut in a "Pignatta," that is, in a high-sided crock pot with a lid.
  - Add plenty of EVO Oil, a couple of cloves of peeled Garlic, 1 medium Onion thinly sliced with a mandoline, some finely chopped Parsley, a pinch of Salt and the Potatoes also thinly sliced.
  - Let it cook for at least two hours on low heat. Remember halfway through cooking to add a half glass of White Wine that you will let fade, then cover the Pignatta again.
  - At the end of cooking, sprinkle with Ground Pepper and if necessary, adjust the Salt.

Anchovies Tarantine style

I know, in the descriptions of these recipes I'm going to sound whiny and repetitive but-what can I do if they are almost all made with simple, easy-to-find and inexpensive ingredients? The fact is that, in this millennium, we often lose our sense of time and no longer realize that, at least Italy (and certain south regions in particular) until about sixty years ago was a predominantly peasant, poor country where life and traditions had been the same for centuries. People had to make do with what little they had or could afford. And I am talking about those who "something" they could somehow afford. That's right, because there were many who barely, barely managed to get a piece of bread. Yet, thanks in part to the geographical and climatic features of this beautiful land, our ancestors and forefathers still managed to come up with tasty and nutritious recipes. As anyone who has ever tasted them can safely testify. No doubt about it!

Difficulty: Easy - Preparation: Quick - Cost: Moderate

What You Need (For 4 people):
- Fresh anchovies/anchovies – 2.2 lb
- Extra Virgin Olive Oil (EVO)
- Salted capers - About 20
- Oregano (either fresh or dried is fine)
- Basil leaves - 4 or 5
- Dried chilies - 2 or 3
- Pitted olives - About 20
- Tomato sauce – 0.5 lb
- Dry white wine
- Salt

How to Prepare:
- First, if you have not had the fishmonger clean the Anchovies you will have to do it yourself. Then wash them thoroughly under running water, scrape the outside lightly with a smooth-bladed knife, cut off the head and fins and then open them in two. Discard both the entrails and the central spine.

- Give the resulting fillets another rinse under water and then arrange them in a suitably sized Pyrex dish. The inside should be oriented upward. Add plenty of EVO Oil and a pinch of Salt.

- Now prepare a fine Chop with the Chili, Capers (desalinate them first in a glass with warm water), Basil, Olives and Oregano.

- Now cover the Anchovies with the Tomato Sauce and sprinkle the same Sauce evenly with the Mince. At this point, add a glass of Dry White Wine.

- Heat the oven to 360 °F and bake for 25 to 30 minutes.

- Serve them nice and hot.

Gratinated Anchovies

I'm not saying anything-Just did it all in the previous recipe.

Difficulty: Easy - Preparation: Quick - Cost: Moderate

What You Need (For 4 people):
- Fresh Anchovies - At least 4 per person.
- Extra Virgin Olive Oil (EVO).
- Dry bread – 7 oz
- Grated aged cacioricotta cheese – 2.8 oz
- Garlic - 1 or 2 cloves
- Dry white wine
- Parsley
- Ground pepper
- Salt

How to Prepare:
- For the cleaning and preparation of the Anchovies, I refer you to the previous recipe (leave the tail on, however).
- In a large bowl put the Bread (which you will have previously soaked in warm water and then squeezed well), the Cacioricotta cheese, Garlic (peeled) and Parsley (only the leaves) finely chopped, a little Salt and Pepper, two tablespoons of EVO Oil and the White Wine (half a glass)
- Mix everything well to form a well compact but not dry mixture.
- Prepare one (or more, depending on the number of Anchovies) baking pan with baking paper. Then, with a kitchen brush, brush the Anchovies with EVO Oil on both sides.
- Now, for each Alice, scoop out a little of the mixture with the other ingredients with a spoon, place it in the Baking Tray and lay the wide-open Alice on top. Cover it with another spoonful of mixture and with your fingers, shape it to form a kind of meatball, leaving out only the tail.
- Heat the oven to about 390 °F and bake the Anchovies for 15 minutes. When done, 1 or 2 minutes with the Grill on will give the topping an extra crunch.
- Remove from the oven and serve directly on a platter.

Gallipoli's Scapece

More than a recipe, the Scapece Gallipolina is a curiosity, but nothing prohibits you from trying to make it at home as well. It is in fact a method created to preserve food for a long time. In the case of Gallipoli, of course, the most available food has always been that coming from the sea and in particular that of the very small fish locally called "Pupidd" with which excellent fried foods were made. To prepare Scapece, once the small fish were fried (keeping the different types separate), they were stored inside capacious wooden vats between layers of bread crumbs soaked in Vinegar and Saffron. Since you will not be preparing significant quantities, if you do not find small tubs to use specifically, you can always "fall back" on the common hermetically sealed glass "jars" to put then in the refrigerator.

Difficulty: Medium - Preparation: Medium - Cost: Content

What You Need:

- One and a half kilograms of small sea fish (often known as "Fry")
- Plenty of Breadcrumbs (At least 2.2 lb) If you want to make it yourself, use stale bread and grate it after removing the crust.
- Extra Virgin Olive Oil (EVO) for frying.
- White Wine Vinegar – 16.9 oz
- One sachet of powdered saffron

How to Prepare:

- First wash the Little Fish well, then fry them in plenty of EVO Oil. When they are golden and crispy, take them out with a skimmer and place them on paper towels.
- Mix the breadcrumbs with the Vinegar and Saffron.
- Dip the Fried Little Fishes in the resulting mixture and place them on a tray.
- Now place a layer of the same mixture on the bottom of the container you have decided to use for storage. On top of the mixture place some of the fried fish. Continue in this way, alternating the layers.
- When finished, close the glass jar or if you have used the wooden vat, cover it with plastic wrap and store the container in the refrigerator.

Braised Eel (or Capitone)

This is a typical Christmas dish, which is traditionally eaten by families during the "Supper" on Christmas Eve. I still have vivid memories of one of these gatherings, on a very cold evening, with far more relatives than our little „Trullo" house could contain... Yet, it was a happy evening, enlivened among other things precisely by an excellent barbecued eel.

Difficulty: Medium - Preparation: Long - Cost: Moderate

What You Need (For 6 people):
- One 3.3 to 4.4 lb eel
- Wine Vinegar – 6.7 oz
- Extra Virgin Olive Oil (EVO)
- Breadcrumbs – 5.3 oz
- Rosemary (a couple of sprigs)
- 2 Lemons
- Ground Pepper
- Salt

How to Prepare:
- Wash and clean the Capitone well, removing the skin as well. If you are not capable, have the fishmonger do it directly.
- Cut it into pieces of 2 to 2.75 in (also adjust according to the number of diners and the size of the individual Eel).
- Place the pieces in a large container in which you will have mixed the Vinegar with the juice of the Lemons, a couple of tablespoons of EVO Oil, Salt and Pepper. Cover with a lid or food wrap. Leave to marinate for about 3 hours.
- Once the marinating is over, you can cook the Capitone directly on the grill, taking care to turn it often and brush it with the marinating liquid itself. Traditionally, Rosemary branches are used to do this. If you can't prepare it on the grill, use the Oven at about 390 °F for 25 to 30 minutes, always turning and brushing the pieces frequently.

Holiday Sweets

Le Cartellate (I Cartiedd')

A Classic! The most typical dessert of the Christmas tradition, as always made with a few simple ingredients readily available locally. They take this particular name (perhaps) from the Greek "Kartallos" - Basket. They are absolutely not-to-be-missed sweets for lovers of Apulian Cuisine. They are prepared in different variants (the most common is the one with honey) and here I propose the most "typical" of all: Cartellate al Vincotto (made by cooking the must of some typical Apulian vines such as Primitivo di Manduria, Negroamaro and Malvasia). Practically-a drug!

Difficulty: Medium - Preparation: Long - Cost: Moderate

What is needed:
- 00 flour – 1.8 lb
- Extra Virgin Olive Oil (EVO) – 5.9 oz
- White wine (dry) 1 glass
- Vincotto – 8.5 oz
- EVO oil for frying

How to Prepare:
- First, place the flour on the work surface to form the classic cone hollowed out in the center.
- Begin by pouring the EVO Oil into the hollow and then some of the Wine and knead the dough so that it is firm, smooth and not sticky. If necessary, gradually add more wine.
- Divide the dough into 3-4 separate parts and flatten them with a rolling pin until you get the respective sheets. These should be not too thick (two or three millimeters).
- Now, using the classic toothed wheel, create a series of strips of dough, 5.9 to 7.9 in long and 1.2 in high.
- Now you will have to fold the individual strips in two, and with your fingers you must join the two parts, "stapling" them together at regular intervals. This will result in places where the two parts of the strip are joined and others where they are separated.
- Once you have finished the previous operation, roll the strips on themselves, so as to obtain the typical final wheel shape.

- In a pan with plenty of boiling oil for frying, now dip the Cartellate for a few minutes (turning them a couple of times) until they take on a golden and crispy appearance.

- Once fried, let the Cartellate cool on top of a tray with paper towels.

- Fluidify the Vincotto by heating it in a pan and then dip the now-cooled Cartellate one by one, turning them on both sides until they are well coated with the liquid. Lay them on a tray and let them rest for a few minutes.

- That's it, the Cartellate are ready to be enjoyed to the utmost satisfaction of your palates!

Easter Taralli

After Cartellate, a sweet symbol of Christmas, here are the Frosted Taralli that take us into the Easter season. And even more than the former, the latter were never missing from the Easter tables of my "endless" relatives. I don't know why, since they are actually very simple sweets, but in the imagination of us children they always aroused an overwhelming desire for... possession. Could it have been because of the frosting?

Difficulty: Medium - Preparation: Medium - Cost: Moderate

What is needed (Taralli):
- Flour 00 – 1.65 lb
- Extra Virgin Olive Oil (EVO) – 2.5 oz
- Eggs
- Sugar – 3.5 oz
- Bicarbonate of Soda - ¼ teaspoon
- Edible Alcohol - 1 teaspoon
- Salt

What is needed (Icing):
- Sugar – 1.65 lb
- 2 Egg whites
- Water – 6.8 oz
- Half a Lemon

How to Prepare:
- We begin to prepare the Taralli by arranging the Flour on the work surface to form a nice hollowed out cone in the center.
- We now pour the first half of the Oil into the Flour and begin to knead.
- Gradually, we add the yolks of the 6 Eggs, the other half of the Oil, the Alcohol, the Salt (a pinch), the baking soda and the Sugar.
- We continue processing the dough until a smooth consistency is obtained.

- Now we divide the resulting dough and give the different parts a roughly cylindrical shape (1.6 to 2 in diameter). We close the ends so as to obtain a circular shape of the individual Taralli.

- Let us soak (one at a time) the Taralli in boiling water until they come to the surface, then drain them and lay them on the pastry board. Cover them with a cloth and let them rest for a few hours. Check that they dry thoroughly.

- At this point, let's bake the Taralli for half an hour at 360 °F. Once ready, let's take them out of the oven and let them cool.

- It's time to prepare the icing.

- First let's whip the egg whites, then put the Sugar in a pan (or pan) and, once melted, let's add them, together with a few drops of lemon juice and mix until we get a nice homogeneous mixture.

- Now we can cover (completely) the taralli with the glaze. This can be done either by dipping them directly into the pan or by spreading the icing with a brush.

- Let them cool. And there our tasty taralli are ready to be enjoyed.

Purceddhri

The Purceddhruzzi, Purcedd' or one of the other countless linguistic variants that prevail depending on the country in which they are prepared, are yes a typical sweet of Salento, but actually widespread throughout the Apulian territory. Obviously - ça va sans dire - children are crazy about them, but adults are no joke either!

Difficulty: Medium - Preparation: Medium - Cost: Moderate

What You Need (For 5 people):
- 00 flour – 1.1 lb.
- Dry white wine – ½ Glass
- 1 Orange (variations: lemon or tangerine)
- Extra Virgin Olive Oil (EVO)
- Italian Acacia honey – 1.1 lb
- Salt
- Colored cake beads
- Shelled pine nuts (optional)
- Cinnamon powder (optional)

How to Prepare:
- Prepare the "usual" fountain of Flour on the work surface.
- Pour into the flour a couple of tablespoons of Evo Oil, the Stirred Wine and a pinch of Salt. Start working the mixture. Add more Oil if necessary.
- After kneading thoroughly, form a nice ball with a smooth, homogeneous consistency. Place it in a tray and cover it with a cloth. Let it rest for at least two hours.
- Divide the dough into small pieces and knead them into "strings" about half an inch in diameter. Now cut the strings into many small pieces about 1 inch long. Give such pieces a round shape. If you want to follow tradition to the letter, place each ball on the back of a grater to give it the characteristic irregular surface.
- Peel the Orange (well washed) and dip the peel in a saucepan with plenty of EVO Oil to flavor it and bring it to a boil. At this point, fry the Purceddhri for a few minutes until they are golden and crisp.
- Drain them well and place them back on a tray with paper towels.

- Now heat the Honey in a bain-marie and once it has thinned, dip the Purceddhri inside.
- Withdraw them from the Honey and place them in a bowl (or divide them into several small bowls) and sprinkle them with the Colored Balls. If necessary, add the Cinnamon and Pine Nuts as well.

The Intorchiate

These braid-shaped "cookies" have many variations (with almonds, with or without grains of sugar etc.). They were divinely prepared by one of my many aunts, helped by her daughter, and in their house they were never missing. Sweet, fragrant and crumbly. When there were some "visitors," here they were appearing on the table, in their large glass jars with airtight caps. Since Intorchiate keep perfectly well for a long time, of course a good supply would follow us when we returned from vacation. In this way there was a period when they acquired "national" fame since, whoever tasted them among our acquaintances, immediately intoned a peana of thanks to the "mythical" Aunt Raffaella, responsible for so much goodness!

Difficulty: Medium - Preparation: Medium - Cost: Low

What You Need:

- 00 flour – 0.9 lb
- Sugar – 4.6 oz
- Extra Virgin Olive Oil (EVO) – 3.4 oz
- Dry white wine – 4.4 oz
- Butter – 2.11 oz
- Beer yeast - ½ sachet (or baking powder).
- Water
- Salt
- Caster sugar – 2.11 oz

How to Prepare:

- In a nice large bowl mix the EVO Oil and Wine, working well with a whisk.
- Sift the Flour and then add it little by little to the bowl. also put a pinch of Salt.
- Knead everything by hand and then add both the softened butter and sugar to the mixture. If the dough is too dry you can add a little water but not too much. Knead some more and then add the yeast as well.
- When the dough is nice and smooth and elastic, divide it into small parts and knead them into cylindrical "strings," about six inches long and maximum 1 cm in diameter.

- Now fold each string in half, take the ends with two fingers and twist them in opposite directions twice to form a small braid.

- Dip the braids in caster sugar and then place them on top of a baking sheet, on which you have prepared a layer of baking paper. This step is not compulsory in fact, we recommend that you still try some of the Intorchiate without the granulated Sugar. They are delicious even this way!

- Bake them for about 20 minutes at 355 °F. Be careful not to let them get too dark. They should be very very lightly browned.

- Then you've just to be sure to thank my Aunt Raffaella and Cousin Carmela!

Mostaccioli (Mustazzule)

I'll end this book with another recipe related to the main Holidays, as if to emphasize once again the true popular and peasant soul of Apulian Cuisine. In fact, the sweets - although always rather simple and cheap - were mainly prepared to celebrate Christmas, Easter and some other local festivities, such as the feasts of the Patron Saint of the various towns (and they kept for a long time). The other days of the year, in fact, there was nothing to celebrate, because life was hard for most of the inhabitants. I still remind younger people that, until the late 1960s, Italy and in particular Apulia, was a predominantly agricultural, poor country with a high illiteracy rate and a rather short individual life expectancy. Women in particular, were raising numerous children and taking care of the house (without electrical appliances and often without even running water) but also working in the fields. It is almost a miracle then that, over time, they were able to come up with such tasty dishes with what little (ingredients and time) they had. Certainly a hand was lent by that Magic that comes from the Land of Apulia: the Climate, the Terrain, the Sea and the Traditions, have provided the products of this region with those flavors and scents that- once tried-become impossible to forget.

Difficulty: Medium - Preparation: Medium - Cost: Moderate

What You Need:
- Flour 00 – 3.3 lb
- Sugar – 2.2 lb
- Extra Virgin Olive Oil (EVO) – 5.3 oz
- Toasted Almonds – 1.3 lb
- Dark Chocolate – 7 oz
- Fig Vincotto – ¼ Gal (you can also use Wine Vincotto)
- Ammonia for desserts – 0.9 oz
- Water – 5 oz
- Cinnamon Powder
- Cloves

How to Prepare:

- Form a nice cone of Flour on the work surface and add 1.5 lb of Sugar, the EVO Oil, a sprinkling of Cinnamon, a few Cloves, the finely chopped Roasted Almonds, the Casterly Ammonia and start mixing everything well. Slowly add the Vincotto until completely absorbed. Continue kneading until the mixture is fairly firm, elastic and not sticky.

- At this point, roll out the mixture until you have a sheet of dough about 1.2 in thick, then divide it, perhaps with the help of square or diamond-shaped "forms," into pieces about 2.75 in each. Arrange the individual Mostaccioli on top of a well-oiled baking sheet dusted with Flour, or covered with baking paper.

- Bake for 20 to 25 minutes in a preheated oven at 360 to 390 °F

- Meanwhile, prepare the Chocolate Glaze by chopping it up and melting it on the stove with a bit of water in a small saucepan. When it becomes liquid, add the 0.7 lb of Sugar that was left aside and stir well until the mixture is stringy. Now remove from the heat and allow to cool.

- When the Mostaccioli are ready, remove them from the oven and cover them with the chocolate icing using a kitchen brush.

- Let cool for a few hours and then you can enjoy your Mostaccioli. I have purposely given them generous amounts because these cakes also keep well for a quite long time in an airtight glass jar.

Dear readers, we are glad you read this book.

To thank you, we have come up with an exclusive Bonus for you!

Download it for FREE right now using this QR Code:

Review this book on Amazon!

We also want to ask you the favor of taking a minute of your time to leave a review. It is very important for us to know what our readers think. This helps us to make better and better products and will also help al.tri readers in their choice.

Recommend or gift this book to your friends!

Notes

[S] **Special Italian Rices:** https://i-best-magazine.com/speciale-cinque-risi-italiani-top/
[1] **Marcel Proust** https://it.wikipedia.org/wiki/Alla_ricerca_del_tempo_perduto
[2] **Funghi Cardoncelli** https://it.wikipedia.org/wiki/Pleurotus_eryngii
[3] **Mipaaf** https://www.politicheagricole.it/flex/cm/pages/ServeBLOB.php/L/IT/IDPagina/398

Image Credits

Introduction – 1:Image source: by Alessio Roversi on Unsplash
2: Pixabay - No attribution required
3: Pixabay - No attribution required
4: Pixabay - No attribution required
5: Pixabay - No attribution required

Ch. Mussels - Image source: Food photo created by freepik - www.freepik.com
Ch. Bread - Image source: p.berto - Unsplash
Ch. Primi - Image source: pixabay by pixel1 - No attribution required
Ch. Vegetables - Image source: by jordi pujadas on Unsplash
Ch. Meat Dishes - Image Source: Pixabay - No attribution required
Ch. Fish Dishes - Image Source: Pixabay - No attribution required
Ch. Desserts - Image Source: florixc is licensed under CC0
Front Cover Cover - Image Source: Foto di Volker Glätsch da Pixabay - No attribution required
Back Cover - Image Source: Pixabay - No attribution required

About the Authors

Aurora Zito

Previously a traveler and contributor to Travel and Food & Wine Magazines, she is now a full-time grandmother. Every now and then, however, she returns to Puglia...to keep up the habit.

Karing Ship

Azad Publishing's Frontline Team, thanks to the 20 years of experience in Publishing and Communication of many of its members, produces quality manuals and guides (if necessary, with the collaboration of selected outside experts) to meet the needs of discerning readers.

Other Italian Cookbook from the same Publisher

Grill It The Italian Way

Taste Something Unusual and Make your Neighbors Drool with these Mouthwatering Mediterranean BBQ Recipes

Check it at Amazon using this Qrcode

Printed in Great Britain
by Amazon